MONEY
MADE
EASY

MONEY MADE EASY

A SIMPLE GUIDE FOR
Accumulating, Spending
& Protecting Your Money

KEVIN MACLEOD CFP, RRC, CEA

HOUNDSTOOTH
PRESS

Copyright © 2022 Kevin MacLeod
All rights reserved.

Money Made Easy
A Simple Guide for Accumulating, Spending & Protecting Your Money
ISBN 978-1-5445-3284-4 Hardcover
978-1-5445-3282-0 Paperback
978-1-5445-3283-7 Ebook

CONTENTS

Introduction vii

PART III **PROTECTING YOUR MONEY**

INTRODUCTION

Chances are, someone is cheating you out of your money. Without understanding some of the ways that banks, financial institutions, and shady financial advisors operate, you could be paying for products or services that you do not need or want, or that are ticking time bombs.

I recently met a woman in her late twenties who purchased an insurance policy and opened a tax-free savings account from someone calling himself a financial advisor. The insurance policy was sold as a great place to invest her extra money for a rainy day while providing a small amount of life insurance if she died. These products were not the best fit for her. She had no dependents and no real need for life insurance, but even if she did, she could have purchased the life insurance for less than half the cost of this policy. Furthermore, the extra money she deposited into the policy for investment purposes would be quite challenging to get out for a rainy day. She couldn't just withdraw the money. Rather, she would have to borrow money from the policy and then pay it back with interest. She could opt to cancel the policy, but that would mean paying taxes on any gains the investment made. Plus, canceling the policy in the first few years would create a "surrender charge" that would wipe out the savings in the plan. The only efficient way that her insurance policy would pay out the investment portion would be if she died—so someone else would get the money. That is the purpose of life insurance, not short-term investments.

The tax-free savings account the advisor sold her was an expensive (high-fee) investment fund from an insurance company; he didn't recommend it because it was the best option but because it was all he was licensed to sell. She paid expensive fees for guarantees that she will not use and does not need. There is nothing wrong with the investment, but it's the wrong one for her.

These products cost her a lot of money—money that she cannot afford to lose. At first, she was embarrassed that she had made these decisions, but then she was outraged. She trusted this person to give her good advice and direction, but this advisor was motivated by the commissions he was earning, not by the help he was giving her.

The problems faced by this young woman are common. Anyone can call themself a "financial advisor" regardless of their experience or education. For example, a person may be licensed only for life insurance and accident and sickness products. But that person can still call themself a "financial advisor." They can even sell some types of investments, regardless of whether they know anything about investments. They can portray themself as knowing how to create and protect wealth when all they may want to do is sell you a complicated life insurance scheme that pays them high commissions. These insurance schemes are ticking time bombs and are usually entirely inappropriate for the average middle-class people who get sucked into them.

However, when you are informed and aware of how banks and bad advisors can take advantage of you, either by not giving you the correct information or by leading you down a financial path of destruction, you will know what to look for, and you can fight back.

With this book, I give you the tools so no one can cheat you out of your money again.

Learn how to tell the difference between a trusted financial advisor and an advisor or bank employee who either does not know what they are doing or, worse, is corrupt or dishonest.

Learn how to maximize your accumulation of assets.

Learn how to spend your money properly.

Learn how to protect your money, property, and income.

It's easy if you know what to do.

WHY SHOULD YOU LISTEN TO ME?

Let me tell you a story.

When I was in my late twenties, I sold my first business and made a lot of money. I needed advice about what to do with this money, so I went to the bank and asked to speak with a financial advisor. I wanted advice; what I got was a stockbroker. He sold me a stock investment that quickly lost half of its value. Against his advice, I sold it. It would have been worth ten times as much in just a few years if I had kept the investment. The problem was that I had minimal experience with investing, and I did not understand the risk I was taking. The advisor I worked with didn't properly assess the risk that I could tolerate and sold me the wrong investment. The investment was not a bad investment; in fact, it ended up doing very well over time, but I didn't get rewarded because of my behavior.

A few years later I decided to become a financial advisor, to help people create and protect their wealth. While I was very good at running a business, I didn't know much about being a financial advisor. I was recruited by a large insurance company that offered training. I obtained my license to provide investment advice as well as my license to provide insurance advice. I enrolled in the Certified Financial Planner (CFP™) program and obtained my designation in 2001. Mark, my trainer at the insurance company, was (is) someone I now call a trusted financial advisor. Mark was all about helping people; he taught me to concentrate on helping people, not on pushing products. He taught me to educate my clients about money and to help them make decisions. My job was to simplify their world, not to sell them on a bunch of complicated products. Mark taught me that the only way to have long-term success in this business is to be a trusted financial advisor. It took me many years to build my business to a point where it could be called successful, but today I am in the top 5 percent of independent financial advisors in Canada. My team and

I have helped thousands of people grow their wealth and protect their assets.

Let me help you prevent making the wrong decisions regarding your money. I promise to keep it simple and make it EASY!

WHAT IS A TRUSTED FINANCIAL ADVISOR, ANYWAY?

A trusted financial advisor (TFA) is an individual who has not only taken the training and licensing for providing investments and insurance but also holds (or is in the process of obtaining) a financial planning designation such as Certified Financial Planner (CFP™). The most widely recognized financial planning designation in Canada and worldwide, the Certified Financial Planner™ designation provides assurance to Canadians that the design of their financial future rests with a professional who will put their clients' interests ahead of their own. The TFA should also be a member of an industry association that promotes a professional code of conduct that sets out the principles that members are expected to abide by in their business activities and when liaising between clients and suppliers of financial and insurance products or services (associations such as Advocis and the Financial Advisors Association of Canada). A trusted financial advisor is not a designation; it is a way of providing financial advice to clients. A TFA will get to know you and your unique situation, your goals, and your resources to reach those goals and will provide the advice and recommend the products and other services that can help you obtain them.

ABOUT THIS BOOK

This book has three sections:

1. **Making Money.** It is pretty hard to do anything with money if you do not have it. This section will introduce you to taxation, earning, saving, and investing money.

2. **Spending Money**. Learn how to create your lifestyle. Learn how to make big financial decisions and set yourself up for success.

3. **Protecting Your Money.** Life happens, and you can protect yourself and your loved ones from the events that life sometimes throws at us. Plan for the best but prepare for the worst.

Each section is divided into chapters that cover a specific topic. In each chapter, you'll see what a trusted financial advisor would advise in a given situation. I then explain the facts so you'll understand exactly how each product (or financial decision) works. Finally, I'll share some tips about what to watch out for when working with a financial advisor. Then you'll be armed with all the information you need to set yourself up for success.

Are you ready to jump in?

PART I

MAKING
MONEY

CHAPTER 1

INCOME AND TAXES MADE EASY!

LOUSY OUTCOME

Dawn was an employed geologist in New Brunswick who made around $200,000 per year at her regular job. She was offered contract work at another company, which would have paid her about $200 per hour. She wanted to accumulate as much money as possible, so she accepted the contract and made around $150,000 in extra income. She did not need that income to support her lifestyle, but she wanted to renovate her home. Dawn spent $100,000 on renovations. In April, her accountant informed her that she owed an additional (approximately) $80,000 in taxes from her contract position. Dawn knew there would be some additional tax to pay but could not believe that it was over half of what she earned! She did not have the money, so she took out an additional mortgage on her house to pay the taxes.

GREAT OUTCOME

When Dawn was offered the contract position, she called her trusted financial advisor. The TFA asked lots of questions about Dawn's situation and goals, and then explained some important details about taking on contract work. First, contract income is treated as regular income. Second, because she was not an employee, the company paying that income was not required to withhold taxes. The trusted financial advisor calculated the approximate tax in advance of Dawn accepting the contract so she understood how much of the income would go to paying taxes.

The TFA discussed two options for Dawn, both of which would help her avoid being blindsided by a giant tax bill come April.

1. **Dawn could open a corporation**. If she did so, her contract money could go into the corporation account instead of her personal account. The benefit of doing this was that Dawn could control the amount of personal income she took from the corporation. She could take the money out as regular income or dividends whenever she wanted. Small business corporations pay less tax than individuals do (up to the first $500,000 of net income), so more of the money would

stay in the corporate bank account until Dawn needed it.

2. **Dawn could contribute to her retirement savings plan (RSP) and reduce her taxes.** If she did so, she would substantially reduce the amount of tax paid on the extra income she earned. Because Dawn was earning more income that year than usual and may not have had this opportunity again, the use of her RSP contribution room (see Chapter 4) would have helped reduce her taxes and put money away for the future instead of giving it away to the taxman!

Dawn decided to take the contract but held off on the renovation until she knew exactly what money she had left over to spend after tax season.

THE FACTS

To save, spend, and protect your money, you will need to earn money (called income). Making the most out of your income is the subject of this book. You must pay tax on your income, but different kinds of income are taxed in different ways. Tax is unavoidable, but with proper planning and advice, and by understanding how income is taxed, you may be able to pay less!

Income is earned in the following ways:

1. **As an employee:** When you trade your time

or mind for money, a business owner pays you for the tasks you perform. You get paid a regular wage or commission, and the employer is bound by law to withhold income taxes and follow labor laws of the province where you are employed. Employment income is taxed as regular income. Note that some contract workers are not "employees," and therefore they do not have taxes withheld by their employer. This income is still taxed as regular income.

2. **As a business owner:** You provide goods or services to customers, and those customers pay you. You pay the expenses to run the business, and you get to keep what is left. This kind of income is taxed as regular income. You are required to calculate and remit your taxes owed to the government.

3. **As a landlord:** If you own a property or the rights to a property, you can charge someone a fee to stay there or use the property. This is called "rent." Rent is taxed as regular income (unless it is your business to rent things to others).

4. **From savings:** This is the money paid to you when you save your money in an account that pays "interest." Interest is like rent. When you open a savings account, you're actually lending your money to a bank or credit union, and it pays you back a percentage of your money for

as long as it has it. For example: if the "interest rate" is 1 percent and you have saved (lent to the bank) one hundred dollars, then it will pay you one dollar of interest after one year. You can also earn interest on bonds (discussed in Chapter 2). Interest is taxed as regular income.

5. **As a shareholder of a corporation:** If you own a corporation or own shares in a public corporation, you may earn income in the form of dividends. Dividends are how companies share their profits with the people who own the company. Dividends are taxed at a lower rate than interest or employment income.

6. **When you sell an asset:** You can earn income by selling an asset for more than you bought it for; this is called a "capital gain." If you purchase a rental income property for $200,000 and sell it later for $300,000, you have a $100,000 capital gain. Only 50 percent (currently) of your gain is taxable. So you will pay income tax on $50,000 instead of $100,000, making this a great way to earn income!

7. **As a retired person:** Withdrawals from retirement savings plans or retirement income fund accounts or income from a pension plan is taxed as regular income. You do not pay tax on the money inside the plans (see Chapter 4) until you withdraw it.

ADVISOR WATCH

A trusted financial advisor will get to know the way you earn income to help you take advantage of any tax savings opportunities available to you. The more income you make, the more critical it is to get advice. The last thing you want to do is pay the tax you could have avoided by proper planning.

Some financial advisors are just salespeople. If your advisor or bank teller does not discuss tax planning with you before recommending investments or insurance schemes, you should run away! Trusted financial advisors will only recommend investments or insurance solutions when they know your entire situation as well as your short- and long-term goals.

CHAPTER 2

HIGH INTEREST SAVINGS ACCOUNTS MADE EASY!

LOUSY OUTCOME

Mackenzie was saving for a new car, so she went to her bank and opened a savings account directly tied to her checking account. The amount of interest she would earn was meager, but she liked the convenience of having one bank to deal with. She could quickly move money from her checking account to her savings account anytime. At the end of the year, her $2,500 deposit had made about $5 in interest. When Mackenzie transferred her money back into her checking account to buy her car, she was charged a $10 withdrawal fee by her bank. She was not impressed! She was charged more in withdrawal fees than she made in interest!

GREAT OUTCOME

Mackenzie went online and saw that several banks offered online accounts that pay a bit more interest than her bank but advertised no fees at all. Mackenzie was totally impressed! It took her a bit more work to open a new account; however, once it was open, it was easy for her to move money from her checking account to her new savings account. She earned $62.50 of interest during the year, and when she moved the money back into her checking account, she was not charged any fees at all.

THE FACTS

What do you do with savings that you have accumulated for a short-term goal like buying a house, renovations, damage deposits, or any other lump sum that you know you will need in the future? What do you do with savings that you have put aside for emergencies like loss of income, or home and car maintenance?

The most efficient use of those savings is to place them in a high-interest savings account. You do not have to open a savings account with the same bank that provides your checking account. Having a healthy short-term savings account is an excellent idea for most people to help them accumulate the money they need for purchases so they do not use credit cards or lines of credit that charge interest.

The key to choosing the right high-interest savings

account is to consider the combination of convenience, fees, and interest rate paid. If it is cumbersome to get the money in and out of your regular bank account, the fees would have to be minimal, and the rate offered should be high. Conversely, if the interest rate is slightly lower, but it is easy to transact and there are no fees, that may also be a viable option. The worst option is a combination of high fees, a low rate, and convenience. And guess what! That is likely your bank, so do not hesitate to search away from your main bank for an account with a high rate of interest and low or *no* fees where it's convenient to transact business.

Note: if you have consumer debt, like credit card debt or lines of credit, you should NOT have high-interest savings accounts until those debts are paid off.

ADVISOR WATCH

Most advisors do not get paid much (or anything) to direct their clients to high-interest savings accounts. However, these accounts can be significant parts of a client's financial planning. A trusted financial advisor will align themself with institutions that can offer high-interest savings accounts to which they can refer their clients. That includes making opening the accounts part of their process, whether they get paid to do it or not. If your advisor does not discuss high-interest savings accounts with you regardless of whether or not they offer them, this is a sign that they do not care about doing a complete job for you.

CHAPTER 3

TAX-FREE SAVINGS ACCOUNTS MADE EASY!

LOUSY OUTCOME

Jeff and Laurie were married in their midforties. They inherited some money when Jeff's parents passed away. Jeff and Laurie each made about $30,000 per year in their jobs, so the $150,000 inheritance was a lot of money to them. They were determined to make the most of the money, so they went to the bank and told the advisor that they wanted to invest the money for retirement. The bank advisor introduced them to the tax-free savings account (TFSA). She explained that any money they deposited into the TFSA account could be withdrawn in the future tax-free! That would include any of the income that the investments inside the TFSA made. Jeff and Laurie told the advisor that they wanted the money to grow but did not want any risk, so the advisor recommended a five-year guaranteed investment certificate that paid about 2 percent (see Chapter 11). After five years they had a grand total of $165,612.

GREAT OUTCOME

When Jeff and Laurie inherited the money, they realized that they did not know what to do with it and asked their neighbor and good friend to refer them to a trusted financial advisor. The TFA asked Jeff and Laurie many questions and determined that Jeff and Laurie genuinely wanted to honor the inheritance by funding their future retirement. She introduced them to the tax-free savings account. She also educated Jeff and Laurie on how to invest for the long term and, once she established their risk tolerance, recommended a medium-risk investment fund (see Chapter 7). After five years they had a grand total of $200,734. By investing the funds appropriately, Jeff and Laurie made an additional $35,000.

THE FACTS

In 2009 the federal government introduced the tax-free savings account.

The TFSA is an account that you fund with after-tax money. After-tax money is money that you either earned from employment or business and on which you already paid the tax (see Chapter 1), or money that you have that did not attract tax in the first place (an inheritance, lottery, low income, etc.). Once the money is deposited into the TFSA, any future withdrawals, including any investment gains, are completely tax-free!

A TFSA is not an investment; it is an account that holds investments. The types of investments allowed in a TFSA are mutual funds (see Chapter 7), publicly listed stocks (see Chapter 5), government bonds (see Chapter 6), certain corporate bonds (see Chapter 6), ETFs (see Chapter 8), GICs (see Chapter 11), high-interest savings accounts (see Chapter 2), and options (too complicated for this book!).

A TFSA can be a very effective savings vehicle for almost anybody!

People with low incomes who have extra money to save can use the tax-free savings account to accumulate money for the future knowing that the income or withdrawals from their account will not affect any social services for low-income people. People with incomes under $50,197 are already paying the lowest federal tax rate, so a retirement savings plan (see Chapter 4) may not be the ideal savings vehicle as future withdrawals are taxed and may possibly affect social benefits for those with lower income.

People who are not considered low income can also effectively use the TFSA for future accumulation. In Canada, the more money you make, the more tax you pay. So accumulating money in a TFSA means that any future growth or withdrawals will not put you into the next level (tax bracket) of income tax.

There are rules and limits for tax-free savings accounts.

Canadians can deposit after-tax money into their tax-free savings account up to their contribution limit. You can have as many TFSAs as you wish, but your contribution limit applies to the sum of all of your deposits into these accounts, not each account separately. Be careful not to exceed your limit. Do not overcontribute. You will be penalized at 1 percent of your overcontribution amount MONTHLY until you withdraw it.

The annual deposit limit has changed over the years. In 2009 the annual deposit limit for adults was $5,000. In 2021 the annual deposit limit was $6,000. The accumulated limit for people who were eighteen or older in 2009 is now $81,500 (in 2022). Your limit is based on your age and what you have deposited or withdrawn over the years. You can request your limit from the Canada Revenue Agency (CRA) website, https://www.canada.ca/en/services/taxes.html.

It is important to know that you can redeposit any amount you withdraw from your tax-free savings account in the year or years following the current year. For example, let's say your limit in 2020 was $30,000. You fully invested $30,000; it had grown to $35,000, so you withdrew the full balance in November of 2020. In 2021, you could recontribute the $35,000 *plus* the new contribution allocation for this year (2022), which is currently $6,000, or $41,000 total.

The tax-free savings account is a powerful savings tool that can significantly increase your wealth if appropriately used.

ADVISOR WATCH

Banks tend to do the worst job of educating clients on the proper use of a TFSA. Most people come out of the bank with a TFSA in a high-interest savings account because people associate the SA in TFSA to mean "savings account." What it should really be called is a tax-free *investment* account. Banks will also often promote a TFSA to bundle the services that the bank has for each customer. Some bank representatives are evaluated by the number of products that they open for customers. A TFSA is just another product for them to add to your list. The bank will often reduce or eliminate your banking fees if you have more than one product with it. This is actually a smart thing for people to do, but the wrong way for it to be done. If you can get free banking by opening a TFSA, do it. Put fifty dollars in and let it sit there. Do your actual TFSA investing properly somewhere else.

CHAPTER 4

RETIREMENT SAVINGS PLANS MADE EASY!

LOUSY OUTCOME

Devin was single, lived in Ontario, and had a stable job that paid him a salary of $100,000 per year. He paid an average tax rate of 27 percent of his income, which meant he took home about $6,000 per month. Devin could live comfortably on this income but did not save any of it for the future. He got a raise of $10,000 per year and began taking home just over $6,500 per month, which meant that almost half of his raise went to taxes. Devin increased his lifestyle and still did not save anything for the future.

GREAT OUTCOME

When Devin got a raise and saw how much extra tax he was paying, he reached out to a trusted financial advisor that his friends recommended to him to see what he could do to reduce his taxes. The trusted financial advisor showed Devin that if he deposited his extra $500 per month into a retirement savings plan instead of spending it, he would get a tax refund of $2,600 each year. So not only would he be saving for the future, he could also increase his lifestyle a little bit as well. If Devin kept saving $6,000 per year (invested properly), he could have almost $100,000 in savings in just ten years.

THE FACTS

A retirement savings plan (RSP) is one of the most widely used and least understood savings vehicles available to Canadians. You can contribute up to 18 percent (to a limit of around $28,000 in 2021) of your annual employment income to an RSP. So if you earned $100,000 in 2021, you would have created $18,000 of available contribution room. You accumulate your contribution room throughout your lifetime. You can use the contribution room for any year. If you do not use your current year's contribution room, it accumulates until you are ready to use it.

Retirement savings plans are savings vehicles to supplement your income in retirement. An RSP can be used to lower your taxable income now and be withdrawn in the future when your income is lower, even if you are not retired. When you place money in an RSP, you have decided to pay the income tax on that money at a future date instead of today.

So let's say that you earn $50,000 per year. Without deductions, you will pay somewhere around 16 percent of that in tax (using Alberta, for example; all provinces are slightly different), so about $7,900 of income tax.

If you saved $5,000 into your retirement savings plan in the same year, your new taxable income would be $45,000, and your new tax would be closer to $6,524, so you would pay $1,376 less in taxes that year.

In Canada, as your income increases and passes specific "tax brackets," the higher the percentage of tax you will pay on that income. For example (Alberta tax rates), if you were earning $200,000 of taxable income, you would pay approximately $62,680 in taxes, which is an average rate of 31 percent tax. The tax rate on the portion of income over $157,000 is actually 43 percent! If you saved $20,000 into an RSP, your tax bill would be $54,208, a savings of $8,400 in tax. So you can see that the higher your income, the more the RSP becomes attractive as a savings vehicle.

The retirement savings plan is not an investment; an RSP is a structure. Within that structure, you can put the money into a range of eligible investments. While the money is in the RSP account, there are no taxes on the interest, dividends, or capital gains earned (hopefully) in the investment account.

So what happens when I withdraw money from my RSP?

You will pay the tax on any withdrawals from the RSP account. Retirement savings plan withdrawals are considered income. RSP income is added to any other income that you earned, and you will pay tax based on your entire income for the year.

Withdrawing RSP money while employed and earning income should be avoided if possible and only done if there is no other option for you. You could end up paying more tax on this income than you saved when you put it into the RSP.

Some programs, such as the Lifelong Learning Plan and the Home Buyers' Plan, allow you to borrow from your retirement savings plan without tax. Speak to a trusted financial advisor to learn more about these excellent programs.

ADVISOR WATCH

Banks are notorious for taking RSP deposits without really asking the right questions. We see this when we take clients who have previously done business with the bank. We see people who earn less than $50,000 per year deposit money into an RSP just for the short-term tax savings. We see young people saving for short-term goals depositing money into RSP accounts only to be shocked by how much tax they have to pay when they withdraw the money. We see RSP deposits that are meant for retirement income invested into short-term investment vehicles because no one asked the right questions. Questions like, "How much money do you make? How many years will it be before you require this money for spending? What is the purpose of the money in the future?" Simple questions that can make all the difference to the success of the client.

CHAPTER 5

STOCKS MADE EASY!

LOUSY OUTCOME

Cale watched a lot of business news on the internet and television. He enjoyed hearing about the economy and about up-and-coming companies and new innovations. Most of the commercials on the business news channels were about new companies looking for investors or companies promoting their future plans in hopes that more people would want to buy shares in their companies. There were segments that promoted stock-buying strategies that claimed to help investors "time the market" (know when a stock's value was about to go up or down so they would know when to buy or sell it), which in reality was impossible to do with any consistency. Cale bought and sold stocks based on what he saw or heard on the news. Sometimes he made the right choice and the stock made money, and sometimes he made the wrong choice and he lost money, which sounds an awful lot like gambling!

GREAT OUTCOME

Cale subsidized his intake of news from the internet and television with the Canadian Securities Course, which gave him the education and ability to accurately assess company, industry, and market performance. It introduced him to and provided him with the skills, knowledge, and tools to help him make more informed choices for the stocks he wanted to buy. Cale still made the odd bad decision, but instead of trading his stocks based purely on the "noise" from the internet and news channels, he started making more informed choices, and his success rate and confidence increased.

THE FACTS

You hear the term "stocks and bonds" all the time, but what does it actually mean?

When a business becomes a "public company," it means the shares (stock) of the company are traded on the stock exchange. Businesses do this to raise money. By selling shares to the public, the current owners of the business get an injection of cash for things like expanding the business, buying other businesses, funding operations, or just pocketing the money. Buyers indicate the price they are willing to pay for the share, and sellers indicate at what price they are willing to sell. The shares trade hands when the buyer's price and the seller's price are equal. The trading of shares happens millions of times a day.

When you purchase shares of a business, you now own a piece of that business—albeit a tiny piece because typically there are millions of shares issued! If the business is successful or the economy is robust, you may benefit because others may be willing to pay more for your shares (if you wanted to sell them) than you originally bought them for. If the business fails or the economy has made the business less successful, others may not be willing to pay as much as you did for your shares (if you want to sell them). The difference in price from when you bought the share to when you sell it is how you will either make money or lose money when investing in stocks. This is called a capital gain or a capital loss.

The business may also pay out part of its profits regularly, either monthly, every three months, or annually, in the form of a dividend. This dividend is paid to everyone who owns the company's shares. You can spend your dividend, reinvest your dividend to buy more shares, or use the money to buy shares of other companies. The dividend is taxable, and you can do whatever you want with it once you get it.

ADVISOR WATCH

Do not base your stock purchases on what you hear from the talking heads in the media. They are there to sell advertisements. Do some research into what kind of businesses you think will do well in the future and make sure you do not have too much of any one thing. Spread your money out over other businesses just in case you are wrong!

CHAPTER 6

BONDS MADE EASY!

LOUSY OUTCOME

Janey wanted to buy a house in a couple of years and had some savings set aside. She was discouraged by the rate of interest that her savings account at the bank made for her, so she told her bank representative that she wanted her money to work harder in an investment that was safe and accessible anytime she wanted it. Even though Janey did not know much about investing, her bank representative encouraged her to open an online investment trading account. The trading account would give Janey access to purchase bonds, which the bank representative explained are just as safe as a bank account and easy to sell when she needed the money. Janey explored all the bonds that were available to her within her trading account. She chose a bond that paid a 5 percent coupon (interest payment) and matured in two years at a price of $100. Five percent sounded good to her! The price of the bond was $125. She bought $10,000 worth of the bond (plus a $10 commission). In two years, her bond matured (paid her back) but she was only repaid $7,990 (including the $10 commission). Over the two years she was paid two interest payments of $400, equaling $800. So she lost a total of $1,220. She thought that she would have made $1,000 (two years at 5 percent of $10,000). She did not understand!

GREAT OUTCOME

When the bank representative suggested that Janey open up an online trading account to choose her own investments, she decided that she did not know enough about investing, so she sought help from a trusted financial advisor that her friends recommended to her. The TFA also suggested that she may have been able to find a bond that paid her more than her savings account and still kept her money safe. The TFA showed Janey how to calculate the value of a bond so she could determine how much interest she would make. When Janey researched the bonds available to her, she looked at the price of the bond, not just the interest rate that it paid. She was able to find a bond (issued by the federal government) that would pay her (after all fees and commissions) around 2 percent per year. Much better than a savings account.

THE FACTS

A bond is a form of debt. Companies and governments sell bonds to raise money. Governments use the money to build infrastructure or fund the country's operation, while corporations use the money to expand or for the company's operation. There are many types of bonds, and within each type of bond, there can be an incredible number of variables or terms. So, for simplicity, I will just be discussing bonds in general.

Bonds are typically sold for one hundred dollars when they become available. When you buy a bond, you lend your money to the government or corporation that issued the bond. It, in return, promises to pay you interest on that money and promise to give you back your money at a predetermined time in the future; this is called the maturity date (a one-hundred-dollar bond matures at one hundred dollars). When the bond matures, you are supposed to get your money back.

Bonds can have very short maturities of only a few months, or long maturities of ten to thirty years or longer.

The amount of interest that you earn depends on two things:

1. The current interest rate environment.
2. The likelihood that you will get your money back when the bond matures in the future.

The more risk you take, the more interest you will get paid. For example, a Government of Canada bond has minimal risk of not paying you back, so the interest rate you will get will be lower than if you lent your money to a public or private company, as that company could go out of business. You might not get your money back.

You can buy a bond one minute and sell it the next minute if you want; the bond market is very active, with billions of dollars traded every day. There is no lock-in period for a bond. Once the bond is issued for one hundred dollars, its value can change instantly. The value or price of the bond will also vary over time.

There are two ways to make money or lose money when investing in bonds:

1. **Interest rate risk.** Suppose you already own a bond that is paying 3 percent, and the Bank of Canada announces that interest rates, in general, are going up. In that case, your bond is less attractive to a purchaser because they can buy a new bond issued and get a higher interest rate. If you wanted to sell your bond, you would have to discount it from the price you paid for someone to want it. The reverse is true; if interest rates decline when you already own a bond, your bond is now worth more than one hundred dollars. You are not required to sell it; you can keep it until maturity, and the interest will keep coming.

2. **Default risk.** If you already own a bond issued by an entity that has since become less likely to pay the interest or even be able to pay you back at maturity, the value of your bond will go down, sometimes drastically. The reverse is true; if the entity seems more likely to pay back

the interest and the principal than it was when you bought the bond, the price you could sell it for will go up!

While there is some risk to bonds, they are generally a safe, low-risk investment, which means they also have low returns (2–5 percent). Although bonds are usually used as part of a long-term portfolio to reduce risk, under the right circumstances, short-term money can be exposed to small amounts of risk to work harder and be more liquid than typical savings vehicles.

ADVISOR WATCH

If you do not know how to find a bond to purchase, you can contact a stockbroker to find the bond for you. You will have to pay that broker a commission to purchase and sell the bond. Most stockbrokers will only purchase individual bonds for clients that have in excess of $500,000. You can buy and sell bonds yourself with an online broker and pay less commission. Most online brokers will have an advisor available who can help you choose the most appropriate bond for your needs. Many advisors recommend bond mutual funds or fixed-income exchange-traded funds (ETFs) for medium-term (two to five years) investment needs. Make sure there are no commissions on the purchase or redemption of the product. These products tend to return low single-figure rates of return, so any commissions paid will deplete much of the gain.

CHAPTER 7

MUTUAL FUNDS MADE EASY!

LOUSY OUTCOME

Bob and Judy were about ten years away from retirement and had accumulated about $500,000. They went to the bank and talked to a planner about options for their retirement savings. Bob and Judy told the bank representative that they did not want any risk in the portfolio as they had worked hard for the money and didn't want to lose it. The bank representative performed a risk tolerance questionnaire with Bob and Judy and recommended the bank's very popular balanced mutual fund. The fund had a fee (represented by the management expense ratio, or MER) of 2.16 percent and had a long-term average rate of return of 6.5 percent annually. After ten years, they would have approximately $900,000.

GREAT OUTCOME

Bob and Judy got a referral to a trusted financial advisor. The TFA asked lots of questions to understand their level of knowledge about investing. The advisor discovered that Bob and Judy knew very little about investing, so she walked them through "Investing 101" and then completed the risk tolerance questionnaire. Bob and Judy answered the questionnaire differently with more knowledge and understanding about risk. The results showed that they had more tolerance for risk than before gaining this knowledge. The trusted financial advisor recommended a slightly more aggressive mutual fund portfolio with a combined overall fee (MER) of 2.08 percent and a long-term average rate of return of 11.37 percent.

In ten years, Bob and Judy would have approximately $1.4 million. That's a difference of $500,000!

THE FACTS

Mutual funds allow greater public access to professional investment management. Before the mutual fund, investors needed a stockbroker to recommend stocks and bonds for their portfolios. The stockbrokers charged a commission for each trade or decision they made. A mutual fund has hundreds or thousands or tens of thousands of people pooling their money together in one portfolio. The mutual fund hires an investment management team that acts as the "stockbroker." Usually, one or two primary portfolio managers drive the fund's strategy, and the portfolio managers are supported by analysts, traders, and administration teams.

When a mutual fund is created, it is typically priced at a value of ten dollars per unit. The unit's value fluctuates based on the stocks, bonds, cash, or other assets owned by the fund. The fund updates its unit price at the end of each trading day. The fund intends to increase the unit's value on behalf of the unit holders. Once the fund is open, it becomes available to be bought by the public. When you buy a fund, you buy it at whatever the current price is at the end of the trading day. When you redeem or sell your fund, you receive the fund's price at the end of the trading day. Your goal should be to sell your units at a higher price than you bought them for. You can buy mutual funds through banks, through online do-it-yourself applications, or through licensed financial advisors.

Even with all our choices for mutual funds, new ones become available each day. Mutual funds are created by banks, insurance companies, and major investment firms such as Fidelity, Mackenzie, or Manulife.

Mutual funds are not free to own. Mutual fund manufacturers and the banks make money by charging a fee called an MER, or management expense ratio. This fee is how they pay for administration, trading, salaries, and bonuses for the fund's management, and for a healthy profit. The MER may also include an embedded fee paid to the client's financial institution or investment advisor that sold or recommended the fund. This fee is called a trailer fee or service fee. This fee is how most financial advisors and bank branches charge for advising their clients. In Canada, a typical mutual fund will have an MER of around 2 percent per year if the advisor fee is embedded or 1 percent if there is no embedded service fee, meaning you're paying 1 percent for advice and service when the fee is embedded. Some financial advisors use funds that do not charge an embedded fee but add a negotiated fee that is disclosed to the client in order to pay for their services. Typically the negotiated fee is equal to or lower than 1 percent (although I have seen advisors charging more than 1 percent, which is hard to justify, in my opinion). The more money you invest with your financial advisor, the more negotiating power you have over the fee you pay them. MERs can range anywhere from 0.05 percent to over 4 percent. Make sure that if you are going to pay a higher fee for your investment, the fund performance and the service and advice you get from your advisor are justified. Banks typically have the highest-fee mutual funds and the least consistent delivery of advice.

You can buy mutual funds that invest in specific assets like real estate, healthcare, technology, or any other kind of asset you can think of. The type of assets in the mutual fund make up the "mandate" of the fund. The fund managers must adhere to the mandate of the fund. So if the fund mandate is real estate, most of the stocks, bonds, or other assets inside the fund must have some connection to real estate. Mutual funds can also have less restrictive mandates such as "global equity," which means the fund managers can buy "equities" (shares) of companies anywhere in the world.

The more specific or restrictive the mutual fund's mandate, the riskier and more expensive it is (in other words, the MER is higher). Conversely, the more generic the fund's mandate (Canadian balanced), the lower the risk and the cost. There are always exceptions to this rule.

A mutual fund with a lower fee than another fund does not necessarily make it a better fund. At the end of the day, the unit holder wants to make a rate of return consistent with the fund's amount of risk. Fund managers can make a significant difference to the performance of the fund. An ideal fund is a fund that has a history of (after fees charged) outperformance against similar funds and its benchmark without taking on additional risk—no easy task.

A qualified trusted financial advisor can ensure that whatever fund you choose matches your risk tolerance. A TFA will also help you manage your expectations about the fund's performance. An experienced TFA is also vital during periods of volatility where your emotions around fear and greed may lead you to make costly, uninformed decisions.

ADVISOR WATCH

Most people who have long-term investments will have money in a mutual fund (or exchange-traded fund, discussed in Chapter 8). The mutual fund world is heavily regulated and going through many changes to better protect the public. Things like commissions, fees, and even ensuring that your advisor knows enough about the fund to recommend it are changing, all for the better to the consumer. Case in point: just recently, the regulators banned banks and robo-advisors from selling mutual funds with embedded advisory fees. So until recently, these financial institutions were scooping up the 1 percent service fee on accounts that are "self-service." It's unbelievable that this went on for so long. There are millions of Canadians paying the 1 percent service fee to banks and financial advisors that do *nothing* to earn it. If you pay a service or trailer fee, you should pay it to the company or advisor giving you some advice. Typically, once the bank or bad advisor has your money in a mutual fund, the communication stops. The next time they will communicate with you is when they see you withdraw the money to invest it somewhere else.

There are thousands of mutual funds available in Canada, so choosing the right one for you can be an intimidating exercise. Not all people licensed to sell mutual funds are "financial advisors"; some are just salespeople for sales organizations that only have their own products to recommend to their clients. You can spot this person because they will be employed by the financial institution and will only recommend that financial institution's products. Even some independent "financial advisors" will just be salespeople that do not offer actual financial planning. Most of the big banks in Canada have banned their "advisors" from selling or recommending third-party (not their own) mutual funds. There is an inherent conflict of interest with advisors recommending only their company's funds; those funds may not be the best of breed and may even have poor performance over other, similar funds.

CHAPTER 8

EXCHANGE-TRADED FUNDS MADE EASY!

LOUSY OUTCOME

Paul was twenty-five, had a steady job, and wanted to invest $25,000 in his tax-free savings account. Paul thought that gold was the next big winning investment, so he looked for a gold exchange-traded fund (ETF) and found the ETF with the symbol HGD. He did not understand that HGD was a leveraged ETF, meaning his gains and losses were amplified by two times on any single day. After three years, his total losses were 53.55 percent as gold prices were down before they were up, and since the leverage amplified his losses, he had much less capital in the fund when it started to go up. Paul could also not regain his contribution limit that the loss eroded.

GREAT OUTCOME

Instead of buying HGD, Paul did a little more research and decided that he would rather not have the risk of the leveraged exchange-traded fund, so he purchased the ETF with the symbol XGD instead. After three years, his average rate of return was 20.04 percent, and his decision to invest in gold turned out to be a good idea; however, he had to live with a period where gold was quite a weak performer. Without leverage, his losses were not amplified, which allowed him to be patient enough to ride out the investment until it made him a profit.

THE FACTS

Exchange-traded funds were invented in Canada nearly fifty years ago and are now one of the fastest-growing products that investors are using worldwide. Essentially an exchange-traded fund tracks the performance (price changes) of a basket of stocks and/or bonds (or other assets) less the fee charged by the manufacturer of the ETF, which is usually relatively low. ETFs are a low-cost way to invest in the stock or bond market.

An exchange-traded fund removes the decisions about which individual stocks, bonds, or other assets to own, making it simple to understand and buy. The value of the ETF will go up or down with the stock or bond market that it aims to replicate. Many trading platforms, such as the bank's online discount brokerage or other online discount brokerages, offer the same ETF; the only difference is usually the fees charged and the services supplied by the trading platform. The fees charged by the ETF provider would be nominal because there are no analysts or other professionals to pay. If you want to buy the largest public companies in Canada, you would buy a Toronto Stock Exchange Traded Fund (such as symbol HXT), which tracks the Toronto Stock Exchange's sixty largest companies.

Supporters of the exchange-traded fund claim that actively managed mutual funds underperform, on average, the ETF that is their benchmark (mutual funds and exchange-traded funds that are the same type and risk level of investment). Still, with careful research, you can find investment professionals who manage mutual funds with a track record of beating the index (even though the fee is higher). Remember that trusted financial advisors can also add value by ensuring that you are choosing the suitable investment to reach your goals, whether that is an ETF, a mutual fund, or a different type of investment.

Like mutual funds, exchange-traded funds allow you to choose to invest in either a general investment mandate (Canadian or international balanced, for example) or a very specific mandate (US small cap, for example) that targets certain industries or sectors. There are also actively managed exchange-traded funds (where individuals or algorithms decide what assets are in the ETF), which is kind of an oxymoron!

The positives of exchange-traded funds are that they are very liquid, can be bought and sold relatively quickly, and are inexpensive to own and trade. ETFs charge lower fees relative to actively managed mutual funds. Unlike a mutual fund, you know in detail what stocks, bonds, or other assets are in your ETF as the manufacturer is required to disclose that information daily. You can choose to buy ETFs on your own through discount or robo-platforms, or you can use an advisor to manage your portfolio of ETFs on your behalf.

The downside of exchange-traded funds is that some can have very complicated structures, so investors should be careful when selecting one. Some ETFs use leverage (borrowing) to amplify gains and losses, which could double or triple your exposure to the underlying investment, which means if you invest $10,000 into the fund, your actual exposure is $20,000 to $30,000. This increases your potential risk and return. Yes, it is complex so best to avoid unless you are a professional trader! If you buy one without knowing the increased risk, you could be surprised (in good or bad ways). Leveraged exchange-traded funds are designed to be traded actively, while other ETFs are better as buy-and-hold investments. Do your research.

Many new "robo-advisor" platforms can help investors choose the amount of risk they are willing to take with their money. The platforms allow for an easy application process to open and manage the account and implement investment suggestions. This technology keeps the costs down as there are no "advisor" fees. However, the lack of an advisor fee also means that there is no advice regarding the account holders' financial situation other than their risk tolerance.

Some ETFs do not have much trading volume. This is important because if you want to sell your ETF, there must be a buyer on the other side, which there always is, but if the trading volume is low, the buyer could be bidding a much lower price for your ETF than the actual value, just like when you are trading stocks. A mutual fund does not have this issue as the fund itself is the buyer and you will always get the end-of-day value (see Chapter 7).

Because most exchange-traded funds are very liquid (easy to buy and sell), they increase the amount of trading that do-it-yourself investors do. But constantly buying and selling the ETF because the investors think they know what will happen next is a great way for them to lose a lot of money. Timing the market is impossible to do on a regular and consistent basis.

ADVISOR WATCH

Fees are not everything when buying an investment, but they are important. Lower fees do not guarantee better returns. If you are paying trading fees for your exchange-traded fund account and you trade often, you could end up paying way more in fees than owning a buy-and-hold, well-managed mutual fund. Exchange-traded funds are easy to buy but not always easy to understand, as evidenced by leveraged ETFs in the story above.

CHAPTER 9

EMPLOYER SAVINGS PLANS MADE EASY!

LOUSY OUTCOME

Darwin started working at the age of twenty-five with a blue-collar company that offered him good pay and a steady job. The company offered a savings plan that would match Darwin's contributions up to 5 percent of his salary every year into a registered savings plan, but Darwin preferred to take his full paycheck. He had just been married and had a child on the way. As Darwin and his wife, Laura, grew older and his salary continued to go up as he got promoted, the family continued to live paycheck to paycheck as they adjusted their spending to whatever Darwin and Laura earned. After twenty-five years, they had no savings to speak of.

GREAT OUTCOME

Darwin and Laura consulted with a trusted financial advisor who stressed the importance of taking advantage of the employer-sponsored savings plan. His employer would match a small amount from each of Darwin's paychecks. Darwin and Laura did whatever it took to arrange their finances to keep up with the program, no matter what. With an average salary of around $75,000 per year, Darwin would have to give up just $320 per month, which when doubled by the employer and invested with a 7 percent rate of return created an account value close to $500,000 when Darwin reached age fifty.

THE FACTS

Some large companies and governments (the "sponsors") provide their employees with pension plans to help them save for retirement. These pensions are "defined benefit plans," as employees know what their pension will pay them once they retire. These plans are costly to the sponsors as the sponsors have to make sure that enough money is in the pension plan to provide the retirees and future retirees with the incomes that they have been promised. Because of the cost, these plans are becoming rarer and rarer every year.

The most common retirement savings plan is a defined contribution plan (DCP). A DCP allows the employee to decide the amount they are willing to save from every paycheck as a percentage of their earnings. The sponsor may or may not match that amount of savings, and the employee decides which investment fund (from the choices given to them by the sponsor) to put the savings in. The risk of saving for retirement is entirely on the employee; the sponsor's only obligation is to provide the plan and make the required deposits (if applicable). The sponsor has no future liability.

You must make a couple of decisions when offered this type of plan. First, what amount do you want to save as a percentage of your pay or what fixed amount do you want to save every pay period? If a sponsor offers to match up to a certain percentage or dollar amount of whatever you're putting in, you will want to maximize that. Take the free money! Maximizing the matching contribution should be your number one priority when budgeting. If there are no matching amounts from the sponsor, you will have to decide how much you can afford to save every paycheck, with the ideal percentage to be no less than 10 percent of your salary. The sponsor will often deduct those savings and include the deposit in calculating your tax deducted off your pay. Doing this helps to reduce the tax withheld on your paycheck, which decreases the "pain" of the savings.

Second, what amount of risk do you want to take with the investment?

The sponsor will usually hire a financial services company to administer the plan, like a bank or investment broker or insurance company. The plan administrator will offer a basket of choices for the employee to accumulate their savings.

Typically, you will complete a questionnaire that determines your risk tolerance, and the resulting "score" on your test will determine the recommended investment strategy.

Not taking the right amount of risk is a common mistake—some people don't take enough risk when they are young and just starting the savings plan, and some people take too much risk in the later years when retirement is right around the corner (see Chapter 10).

ADVISOR WATCH

If your advisor does not encourage you to take advantage of any "free" money that your employer is offering and suggests putting your savings with them instead, this is a red flag. Understanding and maximizing employer-sponsored plans should be one of your priorities if you want to be financially successful!

INVESTMENT RISK MADE EASY!

LOUSY OUTCOME

John was fifty-five, married to Joan, and about to retire from the police department. Most of John's colleagues had already retired, so John sought out some advice from a couple of them. Bill, who had retired the year before, explained that John had a choice: he could accept a monthly income for life from the pension fund or take his money out of the pension fund and invest it himself. Bill thought the pension fund was corrupt and underfunded, so he chose to take his money out and invest it in a real estate development company that had been around for twenty years with a perfect track record of making money for its investors. Jerry also retired the previous year but decided to take the monthly income for life because it fit his risk tolerance. John and Joan decided to put their money in the real estate development with Bill. Fast-forward a couple of years later: Jerry was enjoying his retirement and not thinking about money very much. Bill, John, and Joan got a letter from the real estate development company informing them that due to the downturn in the economy, their interest payments were going to stop. A couple of months later, the news reported that the president and most of the board of directors of the real estate company had been arrested for fraud. The company was now bankrupt. Although lawyers were hired and there were some assets left over, John, Joan, and Bill would likely get pennies on the dollar. Both families would have to go back to work to try to recover their losses.

GREAT OUTCOME

After speaking with Bill and Jerry, John and Joan got a referral for a trusted financial advisor. The advisor met with John and Joan to talk about the retirement decision they needed to make. The advisor considered all their assets and liabilities, what kind of life they hoped to enjoy moving forward, and what assets they wanted to leave their kids when they died. The advisor also discussed risk and what could happen with certain investments over time. Now John and Joan understood what to expect from certain types of investments, what could go wrong, and what could go right.

In their circumstance, taking the money out of the pension made sense. Due to some health concerns, John and Joan did not think that they would live exceptionally long lives and wanted to leave as much money as possible for their kids after they died. Pensions only pay until the pensioner and the pensioner's partner die, so there would be nothing left to give to the kids if they died prematurely. However, instead of taking the risk of investing all of their money with one company, they decided to diversify their investments into some lower-risk, balanced mutual funds and exchange-traded funds. While the downturn in the economy a couple of years later meant that their account balances temporarily went down, they understood what they owned, they rode out the storm as their account balances recovered, and they enjoyed their retirement.

THE FACTS

You have probably heard the term "no risk, no reward" before. This term does have some relevance. If an investment has *no* risk, like a bank account, there is very little reward or interest paid relative to other investments.

Everyone has a different tolerance and opinion on risk. What seems risky for one person may seem low-risk to another. Before you take any risk, you must first understand that risk. If you were going to jump fifteen buses on a motorcycle, you would probably understand that if you did not make it, you could get seriously hurt or die, and if you *did* make it, you may become famous and rich! That is a lot of risk, but a very high reward. Would you take that risk?

The same is true for investments. If you knew that the

investment you were going to make could go to zero but had the chance to multiply itself many times over, would you do it? What if the investment you are considering was likely to reward you a moderate amount over time, with some fluctuation in value but with very little chance of losing anything substantial? Would you do that? The risk you take is directly proportional to the potential amount of money or value your investment can lose or gain.

There are two ways to invest money. One way is to lend your money to a bank, government, or corporation that promises to pay you back one day and pays you interest on the money until it does.

You do this by having a savings account (see Chapters 2 and 3) or owning a bond or bond portfolio (see Chapter 6). Lending money is generally a low-risk investment: your money is available on demand and there is no chance of loss of value, but you will likely see a low return on your investment.

The other way to invest money is to buy companies or physical property. You can own your own business and invest your money in making your business more profitable, or you can purchase shares of companies by buying their stock (see Chapter 5). The value of the business you own is determined by the business's profitability now or what the business's profitability should be in the future. You can also own physical property like homes, land, or another real estate asset, either owned directly or owned through a mutual fund (see Chapter 7) or an exchange-traded fund (see Chapter 8). You do this with the hope that the value of that asset goes up over time.

Investing by buying an asset can be more risky than investing by lending your money to others.

Money that is required to be available within a short period of time should *not* be exposed to investments that have risk.

Money *not* required to be available within a short period of time *should* be exposed to investments that have some level of risk.

ADVISOR WATCH

Risk is a four-letter word. People don't want to talk about it. Most people do not understand the risk they have taken until it is too late. The worst mistake people can make is to allow greed or fear to play a part in their investment decision-making. This mistake is hard to avoid. It is almost impossible to remove your feelings from the investment process, but you will have a much better investment experience if you do. Managing expectations is one of the most important jobs your trusted financial advisor has. A trusted financial advisor will educate you on what you should expect as a reasonable reward for the level of risk that you take. If a financial advisor encourages you to make an investment by only focusing on the rewards and not explaining the possible risks, run!

Past performance does not guarantee future results.

Beware of advisors who try to chase the next big thing. Typically, an investment that has done well recently will be the one to disappoint moving forward. Look for products that have long-term stability and performance during good and bad times. Never own too much of one thing, and do not get caught up in the noise of the media or talking heads on TV.

CHAPTER 11

INVESTING MADE EASY!

LOUSY OUTCOME

John and Mary were saving to buy a house. They had about $2,000 per month that they could put toward their house fund; since they wanted to put a down payment of $40,000 on their home, they hoped to have the money saved in twenty months. Then, John heard one of his coworkers talking about a company that was just about to get awarded a new contract; he said the share price would go through the roof in the next two years! John was very excited as he now thought he could get their money saved even faster. John and Mary agreed to buy the shares of this new company, and things were going great. The share price went up, and after sixteen months, John and Mary saw their account was almost at $40,000, so they started looking for a home. It took them a couple of weeks, but they decided to buy a house and sell the company's shares they had invested in to cover the down payment. As it turned out, while they were shopping for a home, the company announced bad news, and the share price went down. Before they could sell their shares, their account had dropped to $30,000. The home sale was postponed, and John and Mary had to save for a few more months.

GREAT OUTCOME

Instead of investing in the stock market (see Chapter 5) in a company that they knew nothing about, John and Mary consulted with their trusted financial advisor and decided to put their money in a high-interest savings account instead. That way, they knew exactly how much money would be available to them when they began their home search after twenty months of saving. When they purchased their home, they had over $40,000 to use as a down payment. Their savings account had even earned some interest over the twenty months they had been saving!

Investing in the stock market or an exciting venture is not necessarily a bad idea, but risking money that you have a short-term need for is.

THE FACTS

Having some extra money and not knowing what to do with it is a fantastic problem to have. When you have this problem, you understand that you need to set aside money for the future to be successful financially. But what do you do with money so it will grow, stay safe, and be there when you need it?

The answer depends on what you need the money for. Your money needs to have a purpose. Without knowing the purpose of the money, it will be challenging to decide how to invest it and make it grow.

Not all of your money has to have the same purpose. Some of your savings could be for a rainy day, and some could be earmarked for important future purchases like homes or cars or vacations! At some point, you may also want to save for creating an income for yourself when you decide that you do not want to work for income in the future—in other words, retirement.

Short-term money for things like rainy-day funds, vacations in a few months, or even purchases planned for a year away should only be invested in short-term savings vehicles, like high-interest savings accounts. You will not earn much interest, but the money will be safe and secure and available when you are ready to spend it. Anything other than an interest-bearing bank account will have risk and fees associated with it, so avoid trying to get fancy or complicated with this portion of your money! See the chapter on high-interest savings accounts (Chapter 2).

The money you intend to spend within the next five years should also earn interest from the bank or credit union. You will be paid a higher interest rate the longer you commit to lending it the money. These instruments are called guaranteed investment certificates (GICs). You can commit to one year or up to five years. Be careful, however, because it is very difficult and expensive to change your mind once you commit. If you are able to cash in the GIC early, you may have to forfeit your interest payments or pay a penalty.

Another way to earn interest and potentially a profit is to own bonds. Bonds can be complicated, but a bond or bond-type product can solve a medium-term savings solution. A medium-term savings goal would be for things like renovations required on a home, new vehicles, or vacations. Getting solid advice from a trusted financial advisor is very important if you decide to invest in bonds. Bonds are not guaranteed, and they do have some risk. See the chapter on bonds (Chapter 6).

Now the fun part! The money for your longer-term goals, such as retirement or for spending on something at least five to ten years from now, can be "invested"! Investing money means that you will be buying an asset with your money instead of lending your money out. In other words, you can purchase parts of businesses.

Businesses that trade on the stock market are called public companies, which means anyone can buy shares of the business. When you buy a company's share, you hope that the share price will go up over time. Your share may also pay you a dividend. Paying you a dividend is the company sharing a portion of its profits with you. In the future, you may want to sell the share and get your money back; that is how you make money. If you buy your share at ten dollars and sell it in the future for fifteen dollars, you have made a profit, also known as a capital gain. You can invest in a single company by buying stock (see Chapter 5), or you can invest in several businesses at once by putting your money into a mutual fund (see Chapter 7) or an exchange-traded fund (see Chapter 8).

The price of the company's shares goes down and up over time; this is called fluctuation. This fluctuation is why the money needs to have a longer-term purpose, as the value will constantly change as the company goes through the ups and downs of business cycles. Your behavior is one of the most important influences on whether you are a successful investor, so you should not do this alone! Most investors have very little stomach for the ups and downs of owning businesses. A trusted financial advisor will help you through the tough times; this is one of their most important jobs!

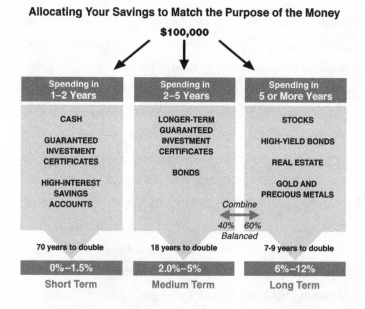

Allocating Your Savings to Match the Purpose of the Money

$100,000

Spending in 1–2 Years	Spending in 2–5 Years	Spending in 5 or More Years
CASH	LONGER-TERM GUARANTEED INVESTMENT CERTIFICATES	STOCKS
GUARANTEED INVESTMENT CERTIFICATES		HIGH-YIELD BONDS
		REAL ESTATE
HIGH-INTEREST SAVINGS ACCOUNTS	BONDS	GOLD AND PRECIOUS METALS

Combine
40% 60%
Balanced

70 years to double	18 years to double	7-9 years to double
0%–1.5%	2.0%–5%	6%–12%
Short Term	Medium Term	Long Term

Other long-term assets that can build wealth for you are things like real estate and precious metals like gold and silver. Real estate (houses, apartments, or office buildings) can earn income if others rent them from you and typically goes up in value over time (the longer the time period, the more likely the value of the real estate will increase). Precious metals like gold and silver do not attract income, so you are only relying on the value of the metal to go up over time.

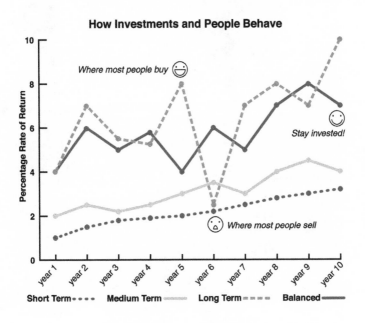

ADVISOR WATCH

A good advisor will know the purpose of the money you intend to invest. If the advisor does not know the purpose of the money or, worse yet, they do not educate you on the risks of making the wrong decision about where you invest the money, you should run away. Advisors do not make much if any money on high-interest savings accounts and GICs. This means that a bad advisor may put short- or medium-term money into something more appropriate for long-term money because they can make more money on the account. Instead of focusing on the needs of the client by doing the right thing, they focus on making money for themselves.

PART II

SPENDING
MONEY

CHAPTER 12

BUDGETING MADE EASY!

LOUSY OUTCOME

Ray and Barbara both had jobs with a regular monthly salary, so they knew exactly how much money they had coming in every month. They had a mortgage structured as a line of credit, so they were only paying the interest on it most months, and the principal was still relatively high compared to the market value of their home. They drove older cars and had two school-age children. Their budget ran tight almost every month, and when they did overspend, they topped up by borrowing more of the line of credit they had against the home. Neither had employer-sponsored savings plans, and they did not set aside any money regularly. They got back a few thousand dollars every April when they filed their tax returns. Barbara loved to travel, so each year they booked an all-inclusive Mexico vacation with their refund.

GREAT OUTCOME

Ray and Barbara got referred to a trusted financial advisor. The TFA reviewed their typical spending patterns and recommended changes. He advised them to restructure their current finances to systematically reduce their debt over time, to reconsider the need for a vacation every year, and to start on a long-term savings plan. After some time, Ray and Barbara saw the light and prioritized the savings rather than giving in to the instant gratification of buying the newest gadget or going out for expensive dinners. Fast-forward a few years: Ray and Barbara had built up significant equity in their home and felt confident that they would someday be able to retire. With their newfound ability to control their expenses, they were able to save for a nice family vacation every year without going into debt.

THE FACTS

The average family has a fixed amount of income every month.

From that income, you must decide how to spend that money. Everyone has all or some of the following that they allocate some of their income to:

1. **Housing**—where you live (rent or mortgage payments)
2. **Transportation**—how you get around (car payments, transit fare)

3. **Insurance**—what you need to protect
4. **Food**—how you eat (groceries, restaurants)
5. **Children**—the costs associated with having kids (education, sports, day care)
6. **Personal care**—haircuts, health clubs, etc.
7. **Entertainment**—what you're doing when you're not at work
8. **Debts**—how much you must pay every month to service your debts
9. **Savings**—what you pay yourself every month
10. **Gifts and donations**—what you give away

How do you decide on how much of your income to allocate to the different aspects of your life?

A truly easy-to-follow and time-tested ratio that I first discovered in the book *The Richest Man in Babylon* is the 70/20/10 rule:

- **Allocate 70 percent of your income to your life-style.** Everyone has a different LIFESTYLE. Some live very simple lives without needing luxuries or expensive vacations, while others emphasize material possessions. There is no wrong answer; both lifestyles can still succeed financially.

- **Allocate 20 percent of your income to reduce short-term or long-term debt**, including any credit cards or loans you have accumulated over time. Another way to use this 20 percent of your income if you have no short-term debt is to accumulate it for short-term needs such as repairs, vacations, or emergency funds. Once the short-term debt has been taken care of, you can allocate this portion of your income to help reduce long-term debt like your home mortgage, over and above your regular mortgage payments. Or you can increase your long-term savings or even increase your spending on your lifestyle. Or even all three!

- **Allocate 10 percent of your income for your future income needs.** This money will take care of your FUTURE LIFESTYLE when you no longer want to work for it. These funds accumulate in your long-term savings vehicles such as tax-free savings accounts, retirement savings plans, or other assets for the future.

When you meet with a trusted financial advisor, budgeting is the first thing you should discuss with them. An advisor can give you advice about supporting your lifestyle while also servicing your debt and saving for the future. We often use a custom spreadsheet to help us organize the household expenses. The 70/20/10 structure is an excellent guideline to managing your life; the ratios are a target, and if you're not there yet, keep working toward the targets. You can also use apps like Mint or Microsoft Money to help track your spending. Doing so can help you identify the gaps preventing you from reaching your target goals. Following this budgeting guideline will help ensure your successful financial future.

To download this worksheet go to http://www.kevin-macleod.com/familybudget.

ADVISOR WATCH

If your financial advisor does not discuss budgeting, it is probably time to find a new financial advisor. Advisors that recommend investment or insurance solutions without knowing your spending habits and cash flow cannot possibly know what is best for you to meet your future goals.

CHAPTER 13

CREDIT SCORES MADE EASY!

LOUSY OUTCOME

S haun was twenty-five years old and single. He had a cell phone account and a credit card from a furniture store. He did not pay much attention to his bills. Shaun only paid his bill when the cell phone company called and threatened to turn off the service. When the furniture store called because his payment was late, he paid the bill. He rarely paid any of his bills on time. Shaun got a raise at work and decided to buy a new car. He went to a car dealer advertising 0 percent interest rates on new cars, picked out his new car, and met with the finance manager at the dealership. After completing his application, the finance manager informed him that he did not qualify for the 0 percent interest rate because his credit score was too low. In fact, if he wanted to finance any car, he would have to pay close to 14 percent interest.

GREAT OUTCOME

Shaun paid his bills on time and when due. His credit score stayed within the acceptable range for most lenders, allowing him to qualify for the dealer's special financing. Shaun checked his credit score regularly to see how potential lenders viewed him as a credit risk.

THE FACTS

If you apply for a credit card, mortgage, or any form of financing, the lender will likely obtain your credit history from the credit agencies (Equifax, TransUnion). Your individual credit score is calculated by the credit agencies from the data they receive from some of the companies you have business with, including city utilities, cell phone and internet providers, and any credit cards or loans you have outstanding. The data sent to the credit agencies is information about the amount of your debt, whether or not you have defaulted on any debts, and whether or not you pay your obligations on time. Your credit score influences the decisions made by the lenders to grant you credit and determine the risk you pose to the lender. If your credit score is low, you may not be successful in getting the credit, or you may be offered the credit at a much higher interest rate. The higher interest rate offsets the lender's risk when issuing credit. You can and should regularly (annually at least) check your credit score by contacting the agencies directly. Both of the agencies listed offer instant credit scores once you have signed up for their service. Credit scores range from 300 to 900 with a "good" score being around 660 and an "excellent" score being above 760. Scores below 660 can make obtaining credit more difficult.

Financing for vehicles, furniture, or electronics is usually relatively easy to obtain, even with lower-than-average credit scores. Financing a mortgage or low-interest lines of credit is challenging with a low credit score. If you maintain an average or above-average credit score, you will likely be granted credit much more easily and at more favorable interest rates.

Maintaining an average or above-average credit score is achieved by:

1. **Paying your bills on time.** Utility companies, cell phone companies, and credit card companies all report your payment history to the credit agencies. Late payments or missed payments will hurt your score.

2. **Closing unnecessary accounts.** Lenders may feel you have too much credit available, which can pose a risk to them if you use it all and fall behind in your obligations.

3. **Not applying for credit you do not need.** Your credit score is "hit" every time you apply for credit. If you have too many 'hits' on your credit file in a short time, your score will decrease dramatically.

4. **Disputing errors on your credit report.** When

you check your credit score at one of the credit agencies, you can see the accounts that report to the agency. If one of the account holders has mistakenly reported late payments or default, you can dispute the error. If you do not check your credit score yourself, you may not see what negatively affects your score.

ADVISOR WATCH

When advising clients with high levels of consumer debt and little or no equity in their home, a trusted financial advisor should advocate paying down the debts before starting a savings plan. The TFA will also coach the clients on increasing their credit score so that when they require credit in the future, it can be obtained easily and at preferred rates of interest. Banks want you to use as many of their products as possible, so bank advisors are incented to make sure you have credit cards, multiple savings accounts, mortgages, and lines of credit. Bank advisors are not incented to make sure these products are actually the right thing for you to have. Credit card companies will frequently offer to increase your credit limit via a preapproval letter. If you do not need the increased credit limit, you should decline it.

CHAPTER 14

BUYING OR LEASING A VEHICLE MADE EASY!

LOUSY OUTCOME

J enny wanted a new vehicle. She went to a local dealer and chose her new car. When she went to the finance office, the finance manager asked Jenny if she wanted to buy the vehicle for $350 per month for eighty-four months or lease the vehicle for $300 per month for sixty months. Jenny thought $300 sounded better than $350, so she decided to lease it. Jenny signed a lease agreement without looking at it very closely. About three months before the five-year lease was over, she received a letter from the finance company letting her know that her lease was about to expire, and that she had the option of giving the vehicle back to the dealer or buying it out and keeping it. She decided that she would return the vehicle to the dealer. After the dealer inspected the vehicle, they sent her a bill for $2,000. She had exceeded her mileage restriction, the car needed new tires, and there was some abnormal wear and tear. Jenny was not expecting this expense at all.

GREAT OUTCOME

Jenny looked over the lease document more closely and saw that she was limited in the amount of mileage that she could put on the vehicle over the five years. Furthermore, the interest rate was higher on the lease than on the purchase. In fact, she would not pay any interest at all if she financed the car instead of leasing it. Jenny decided to purchase the car outright instead of leasing it. At the end of five years, she decided she wanted to buy a new vehicle, so Jenny sold the old vehicle for a little more money than she still owed, which helped her purchase an even better new vehicle.

THE FACTS

Are you thinking about a new vehicle?

Many people like the new-car smell and taking advantage of easy dealer financing to buy or lease new vehicles. Most advisors recommend paying cash for a vehicle that is two years old or older, due to the amount a vehicle depreciates (loses value) in the first few years. You can lease used vehicles or obtain loans for used vehicles but the interest rates tend to be higher than on new vehicle loans or leases.

When getting a new car, you should negotiate the price you are willing to pay for the vehicle first. Do not negotiate payments; negotiate the price you are paying, including all fees and taxes. If you require financing, the next decision you will make is to either lease or buy the vehicle. The payments, whether you are leasing or purchasing, are based on the price that you pay for the vehicle.

LEASING

The main advantage of leasing is that the depreciation of the vehicle's value is the finance company's risk. This is called the residual value. Residual value is the estimate that the finance company believes your vehicle will be worth at the end of the lease. If the actual value is lower than expected, the finance company will lose the money, not you. The reverse is also true. You might be able to sell your vehicle privately for more than your buyout, which is a nice tax-free gain!

Your lease payment is usually lower than your purchase payment due to the calculated residual value. The lower payments may enable you to get a vehicle with more features than buying a car with fewer features and options. You can also change vehicles more frequently as lease terms are typically shorter terms than when buying. And at the end of your lease term, when you're done with the car, you simply give it back to the dealer and walk away. (Conditions apply!)

However, there are downsides to leasing a vehicle. The vehicle is technically not owned by you during the lease term. The finance company dictates what you can or cannot do with the vehicle. You are responsible for any damage or wear and tear that is not acceptable to the dealer, including tires, missed maintenance, and windshield chips or cracks. Often leases will limit the amount of mileage you can drive the vehicle, and exceeding that mileage can be expensive.

At the end of a lease term, there may be hidden fees, whether you return the car to the dealership or buy it outright. If you want to buy the vehicle at the end of the term, you may have to pay for an inspection. An inspection can be upward of $300. If you want to buy your car and you do not have the cash set aside, you may now have to go and find third-party financing, and the rate you will pay may be higher than when you first financed the vehicle. And depending on the lease terms, paying off the vehicle early can be more expensive than it would be if you financed the car.

BUYING

When you buy a car, there are no hidden fees. You know precisely how much the vehicle will cost over the term of the financing, and there are usually no additional fees if you decide to pay off the vehicle early.

Another big advantage is that you own the car from day one. You can do whatever you want to the vehicle and use it for any purpose. If you no longer want the vehicle, you can sell it or trade it in whenever you want. The downside to this is that you're in charge of taking care of it—and finding a buyer when you don't want it any more. Most vehicles depreciate the most in the first two years of ownership, so if you want to sell it during the first couple of years, you could owe more on it than it is worth. Selling the vehicle yourself to a private party will typically net you more money for the vehicle than trading it in or returning it to the dealer. However, it can be intimidating and inconvenient to deal with the public. You must arrange to show the vehicle, let a perfect stranger test drive it, and ultimately negotiate the final price. Sometimes the pain of selling the vehicle yourself outweighs the benefit of the extra money.

If you cannot decide about buying or leasing, it is all about the interest rate. If the dealer offers different financing rates to buy or lease, choose the lowest interest rate option. If the financing rate is at 3.9 percent and the leasing rate is 2.9 percent, you are better off leasing if the hidden costs inside the lease agreement do not offset the savings on the interest rate.

ADVISOR WATCH

The advisor in this case is often the finance manager at the dealership. The finance office is a profit-generating department for car dealers. Dealerships often have arrangements with banks to provide financing to their customers. There may or may not be extra profit (kickback) for the dealer if you choose the bank loan they offer. If you are unsure, you should ask the finance manager outright. Check with your own bank to see if the rate you are being offered is fair. The finance manager will also offer to sell you life and disability insurance to pay off the loan in case you die or become disabled and cannot keep your payments going. This actually protects the finance company, not you. Creditor (bank) insurance is the most expensive kind of insurance you can buy. It is far better to have individual insurance through a trusted broker if you would like the loan covered in case the worst happens. The finance manager will also try to upsell you on additional products like fabric protection, extended warranty, and rust protection. While there is nothing wrong with that, do your research before adding these products, as they are often more expensive at the dealer than at a private provider. Sometimes they're not necessary at all! When I purchased a car a few years ago and declined all the extras offered by the finance manager, the dealer manager called me to see if the finance manager had actually offered me any of the extras, and even though she had and I had declined them all, she was reprimanded by her bosses for not trying harder.

CHAPTER 15

RENTING OR BUYING A HOME MADE EASY!

LOUSY OUTCOME

Shawn and Dawn had been dating for a couple of years and were thinking of moving in together. Both had steady jobs and thought it was time to buy a home as they did not want to miss out on the hot real estate market. Shawn and Dawn got preapproved for a mortgage and bought a home that they both loved. They decided on a five-year fixed-rate mortgage. A year went by; the real estate market had started to cool off, and so had their relationship. Moving in together was not a good idea, and they decided to break up. Unfortunately, neither one of them could afford to keep the house. They had to sell the house quickly and take a $20,000 loss off their original purchase price. They had to pay another $15,000 in penalties to get out of the mortgage.

GREAT OUTCOME

Shawn and Dawn rented their new home together to see if the relationship would work out. When they decided to break up and go their separate ways, they chose other places to live, and there was little to no financial loss.

THE FACTS

When should you buy a home?

It is important to understand that real estate values do not always go up; they fluctuate. Still, like any investment, history has shown that real estate values should grind their way up eventually. There are certain periods when the economy is good and real estate values can go up significantly. There are also periods during very weak economic times during which real estate values can dramatically decrease.

The big question about finding a place to live is whether you should rent or buy. Both options have positives and negatives, so the best decision depends on your situation.

BUYING A HOME

Buying a home can be a good financial investment. When you make mortgage payments, you're paying off the property and gaining equity (your share of the home's value) instead of paying off the debt and therefore increasing the equity for the landlord. Long-term ownership of your home helps to offset inflation issues in retirement as you will likely not have any debt related to the house by that time, thus reducing the cost of shelter when you are living off savings and pensions. If the value of your home increases, you have created additional wealth for yourself!

Homeownership also gives you control over where you live. You can stay or move, and you get to decide what improvements you'd like to make. The flip side to this is that a home requires care and upkeep. You are responsible for repairs and upgrades throughout the time of ownership to keep the asset's value. Maintenance can be expensive and needs to be part of your budget.

There are also additional fees besides maintenance and your mortgage to take into account. Homeowners pay property and other taxes that can increase substantially over time. If you are part of a condominium or strata where every homeowner shares the expenses of the entire development, then you may be hit with extra costs of which you cannot control the timing. There will also be a monthly maintenance fee, which the condo or strata can change. It is expensive and time-consuming to buy or sell real estate, so selling a home soon after buying it can wipe out a lot of any equity you may have put into the home when you purchased it. Expenses such as real estate agent commissions, legal fees, appraisals, and mortgage payout penalties are considerable.

RENTING A HOME

When you rent a home, you have more flexibility. You can up and move anytime you want (with proper notice to the landlord). You can change locations quite easily. No real estate agents or lawyers are required! However, with more flexibility comes less security. You do not own anything and usually cannot make the home "your home." The owner can sell the property, and it may affect your ability to continue to live there. Your rent can increase with each renewal of the lease.

There are also financial pros and cons. If you rent, you don't have to worry about the changing value of real estate, interest rates, or property tax rates. You also don't have to worry about the cost of maintaining the property. If you save and invest the money that would otherwise be paid by the owners for expenses like upkeep and repairs, you can build a nice nest egg! However, you are not building long-term equity or savings with each payment. If you rent the same home for more than five years, you are probably better off buying it.

So how do you decide whether to rent or buy?

Fear of missing out (FOMO) may pressure you to make the wrong decision about renting or buying a home. Take your time and talk about what would happen if you lost your job, your relationship changed, or some other event forced you to change where you live. Would you be able to afford the monthly payment on your own, or would you have to downsize?

What if real estate values go down in the short term? The more stable your situation, the more likely you should own rather than rent. Stability with income, relationships, and location allow you to avoid having to sell when it is not advantageous to do so.

You should consider BUYING if three or more of the following are true:

1. You have a stable job or income source.
2. You have little or no consumer debt.
3. You have some down payment—20 percent is ideal to avoid extra fees.
4. You have a stable relationship with whomever will own the home with you.
5. You have sufficient cash flow to start a savings plan for maintenance or emergencies.

You should consider RENTING if three or more of the above are not true!

ADVISOR WATCH

Buying a home is a major financial decision often taken lightly by people because it is relatively easy to buy real estate in Canada. Done for the right reasons, real estate can be the cornerstone to your future wealth; done for the wrong reasons, it can seriously harm your finances. Your trusted financial advisor should be able to guide you through the decision-making process by providing an unbiased, non-emotionally-attached opinion.

CHAPTER 16

MORTGAGES MADE EASY!

LOUSY OUTCOME

Dan and Rob had high incomes and steady jobs. They went to the bank to obtain a $500,000 mortgage for their new home. The bank offered them a rate of 1.9 percent for five years. That was a great rate, and without looking at the fine print, they signed the mortgage. Dan and Rob had excellent cash flow and wanted to pay the mortgage off as quickly as possible, so after one year, they called the bank and asked how much they could prepay their mortgage without penalty. The bank would only allow them to make a $50,000 prepayment (or 10 percent) of the original mortgage. Dan and Rob had saved over $100,000. They asked the bank why the prepayment allowance was not higher. The bank told them that the rate they got was in part due to much stricter prepayment rules.

GREAT OUTCOME

When offered the 1.9 percent rate, Dan and Rob asked about the details, and because the mortgage was very limited on prepayment options, they decided to shop around with the help of a mortgage broker. The broker found them a slightly lower rate of 1.8 percent at a different financial institution with more favorable prepayment options, including paying off 20 percent per year, doubling up their payments if they wished, and increasing their payments once per year. These were all features the other mortgage did not offer—and that all allowed more flexibility in paying back the mortgage at a faster rate.

THE FACTS

Buying and financing a home can be one of the biggest and most important decisions you make. Done wrong, this can be a very expensive lesson. But done right, it can be the benchmark of your wealth in the future.

Most people will require a mortgage to buy their first home. Most people will carry some form of a mortgage up to and sometimes after retiring. You can even take out something called a "reverse mortgage" that allows you to borrow back the equity in your home during your senior years.

The first step is determining whether homeownership is a good idea for you (see Chapter 15). Once you are sure that buying a home is right for you, engaging an experienced and trusted mortgage broker is the best way to ensure you get the best mortgage rate, terms, and features that are important to you. A broker shops all the lenders for you with one "hit" on your credit file. Going to multiple lenders without a broker can mean that your credit file is checked multiple times. Frequent checks on your credit score in a short period of time can damage your score and make getting a mortgage more challenging (see Chapter 13 for more information on your credit score).

Mortgages can have fixed rates (closed or open) or variable rates. To keep things simple, we will focus on the most common types of mortgages, not special-situation mortgages or private lending.

A fixed-rate mortgage means that the interest rate has been locked in for the mortgage term, typically anywhere from one to ten years, five years being the most common. The financial institution that provided the mortgage cannot raise or lower your rate for whatever period you have chosen. A fixed mortgage can be open or closed. Open mortgages can usually be paid off anytime without penalty. If you have a closed mortgage, you can not pay off your mortgage entirely before the term is up unless you are willing to pay a penalty to do so. These penalties can be very expensive, so make sure you choose a term that most likely matches your intended stay in the home. The rate on the closed mortgage is usually much better than the open mortgage, because it offers less flexibility.

A variable mortgage means that the interest rate you

pay will vary during the term you have chosen. The rate varies with the changes to interest rates set by the Bank of Canada and the individual banks or lenders. You may start with one rate and end up with a very different rate moving forward. A variable-rate mortgage should be used by people who can absorb potential increases in their payments during the term. If you need some certainty about the payments you will be making, a fixed-rate mortgage is likely the way to go. However, if you are comfortable with the cash flow risks of a variable-rate mortgage and the current rate is lower than that of a fixed-rate mortgage, go with the lower rate option. Usually, variable-rate mortgages can be "swapped" for a fixed-rate mortgage if rates start to go up too much.

Penalties for prepaying a variable-rate mortgage (if you move or sell your house) are usually lower than penalties for prepaying fixed-rate mortgages.

When you can finally sign off on your mortgage, the bank will try to sell you life, disability, and critical illness insurance to add to the payment. Buying this kind of insurance from the lender is the most expensive insurance you can buy. You should contact a trusted insurance broker to recommend the appropriate insurance for your situation. You will save money and be insured appropriately.

ADVISOR WATCH

In this case, it is likely that your advisor will be your mortgage broker or bank teller. A referral is the best way to find a good mortgage broker. The most important thing a mortgage broker can do for you is to understand your unique circumstances and recommend the appropriate lender based on those circumstances. The broker should also communicate and keep your application process efficient. Most brokers will have the same lenders and products, so the value they add will be in the customer service that they provide. Brokers will typically find the best combination of features and rates over a bank representative because bank reps work for the bank and can usually only recommend the bank's products. Make sure the mortgage you get has the features you're looking for and not just the lowest rate. Also, as mentioned, the insurances offered by any lender are more expensive and less secure than obtaining insurance through a trusted financial advisor.

CHAPTER 17

CREDIT CARDS MADE EASY!

LOUSY OUTCOME

Deb and Doug got a preapproved credit card in the mail from one of the large, big-box furniture stores in their area with a credit limit of $3,600. The store advertised no interest for thirty-six months on any purchase made on their credit card, so Deb and Doug went shopping! No payments were required, but the entire amount of $3,600 was due at the end of thirty-six months, or Deb and Doug would be retroactively charged 22 percent (annually) interest on the entire $3,600. While Deb and Doug had every intention of putting $100 a month aside for the inevitable bill, they found other uses for the money, and at the end of thirty-six months, they did not have the money set aside. They were shocked to see that they now owed $6,924 for their $3,600 purchase. They not only had to pay the interest charge, but they also had to make high monthly payments to pay off the bill. All they could afford was $100 per month, of which $66 was interest. It took Deb and Doug more than ten years to pay this bill.

GREAT OUTCOME

Deb and Doug decided in advance that they would only spend what they could afford to pay back in the allotted thirty-six months. They sacrificed short-term needs and wants to make sure this bill was paid. At the end of the thirty-six months, they had the funds to pay the bill and did not have any extra charges to worry about or any more payments to make.

THE FACTS

With the advent of loyalty points, using a credit card for everyday purchases has become very popular, and for the most part, getting points or perks for buying things you need anyway makes sense. However, getting into trouble with credit cards is very easy if you do not pay attention to some essential details you need to know.

The most important thing is to do everything you can to pay off your entire balance by each month's due date.

If you do not pay off your entire balance by the due date, your bank will charge interest on your entire balance, even the portion that you've already paid off. In other words, let's say you had a balance of $1,000 on your bill, and the interest rate charged by the credit card is 24 percent annually.

You make a $500 payment, leaving a $500 balance. On your next statement (assuming no further purchases), you would have a new balance of $500 plus $20 interest (24 percent ÷ 12 = 2 percent × $1,000 = $20). So if you do not pay the entire $520.00 by the next due date, you will pay another $10.40 of interest (2 percent × $520 = $10.40). You are compounding your interest charges (paying interest on interest) at 24 percent.

If you must carry a balance on your card, obtain cards with the lowest possible interest rate and annual fee. However, you should prioritize paying off credit card debt. Targeting 20 percent of your income to pay down short-term debt will put you on the path to success (see Chapter 12 on budgets). Here are some additional strategies that can help you tackle paying off your credit card:

- If an introductory credit card is offered to you with a lower rate than your current card and will allow you to transfer your balances from higher-interest cards, you should take advantage of that. Ensure that you cancel the old card once the balance has been transferred to the new card.
- If you have accumulated a lot of debt on your credit cards or lines of credit, it might make sense to apply for a consolidation loan from your bank. A consolidation loan will combine your debts into one lower monthly payment at a lower interest rate. It will also change the way the interest is calculated, which will help you pay it off quicker.

Having too many credit cards or loans open can lower your credit score. A lower credit score affects your ability to obtain further credit, like car loans or mortgages, at favorable rates.

ADVISOR WATCH

High-interest credit card providers like big-box retailers (Canadian Tire or the Bay), finance companies (Fairstone), and the major banks (Visa, Mastercard) send preapproved credit cards to many people, including those who are the least likely to pay off the charges they make before paying any interest (low credit scores). This is how they make a ton of money. Once a person is in debt, the way interest is calculated and the high rate of interest charged make it very tough for the person to ever get the debt paid off. Just because you have the credit available to buy something doesn't mean you should. If you need short-term financing, apply for a low-fee, low-interest major credit card and pay it off as soon as you can. A trusted financial advisor will promote paying off short-term, high-interest debt as a priority over savings. Once the high-interest bad debt is gone, saving for short-term and long-term goals becomes more attainable.

PART III

PROTECTING YOUR MONEY

CHAPTER 18

LIFE INSURANCE MADE EASY!

LOUSY OUTCOME

Chris and Tom had two kids in day care, a mortgage, two car payments, some consumer debt, and enough cash flow to make it all work. Recently, a friend from Tom's work named Barb went to a national insurance sales organization presentation where she "learned" how to use life insurance as an investment; she thought it was such a good idea that she signed up to become an agent for the company. She was encouraged to take this concept to her friends and family and was promised she could easily earn a six-figure income by selling life insurance. Before she was licensed, she set up a meeting with Chris, Tom, and her "manager" to present the concept. Within a few minutes of meeting the couple, the manager suggested that Chris and Tom apply for a line of credit against the equity they had in their home. They were to take this money, apply for a complicated life insurance policy that started very cheap but increased in costs every year, and once approved, put the money into the policy in an investment that would grow over time and that they could borrow against in the future tax-free. Chris and Tom thought very highly of their friend Barb, so they trusted her and decided to go with the plan. Later, they were angry because they realized that they now had another payment (interest on the line of credit) and not enough life insurance to protect their family. The investments within the policy had lost money, and they needed a new furnace. When Chris and Tom wanted to access the money in the policy, they learned that they would have to borrow money using the investments as collateral. Otherwise, they would have to cancel the policy and pay enormous charges to do so. Chris and Tom were confused and angry, and Barb had no answers for them as she had left the business. Barb, Chris, and Tom were no longer friends.

GREAT OUTCOME

Before signing up with Barb and the national sales organization, Chris and Tom asked for a second opinion about their finances from a trusted financial advisor whom their friends had been using for years. The TFA asked lots of questions and clearly understood their financial situation, budget, and future goals. The TFA explained that growing families with many obligations should keep their costs down while ensuring that their families are protected from unforeseen circumstances like early death or major illnesses. With the help of the TFA, Chris and Tom determined that simple term insurance, budgeting, and reducing short-term debt were the best ways to protect their family and grow their wealth. Chris and Tom were relieved and confident that the TFA had their best interests in mind when making recommendations. They decided to stay friends with Barb and not do business with her. Barb decided to stay in her current job when she realized she might not actually be helping her friends and family after all.

THE FACTS

Quite simply, life insurance is a contract between the policy owner (you) and the insurance company. The policy states for a specified premium (the cost or deposit made by you), the insurance company will pay out a specified benefit (face amount) of money upon the death of the insured (who may be different from the policy owner) to a specified beneficiary (the person or organization that receives the benefit). The premium, face amount, and the insured's death all have some measure of guarantee:

1. The premium or cost of the insurance policy is determined when the contract is issued and cannot be changed or altered by the insurance company. (This excludes creditor or group insurance discussed in other chapters.)

2. At the insured's death, the benefit amount the insurance company pays to the beneficiary is

clearly stated in the policy contract and cannot be altered by the insurance company. The amount paid out can be higher than stated in the contract if extra deposits into the policy are made. It cannot be lower.

3. Everyone dies! However, some insurance policies are only meant to be in force for a specific amount of time (term insurance), like ten or twenty years, while other policies are meant to be in force for the entire life of the insured (permanent insurance). The proper type of insurance must be purchased for the proper purposes!

4. You must be relatively healthy to buy life insurance. When you apply for life insurance you will be asked to provide a history of your health. The insurance company will determine if your health, as it stands right now, will lead you to live less than, equal to, or more than life expectancy. In Canada the life expectancy of a male is around 79.8 years and females are 83.9 years. If you have a history of poor health, such as high blood pressure, diabetes, or cancer, you may not be able to obtain life insurance at favorable rates or at all. The worse your health history, the higher the price. This is called a "rating." When you apply for insurance, you are normally advised of the standard (normal) price.

Standard price is the price most people will pay who have normal or near normal health history. If your health is abnormally poor, the insurance company may still offer to insure you but will offer the insurance to you at a higher price. Ratings can be as low as an additional 25 percent of the premium to up to 400 percent of the premium. For example, if the standard premium is $100 per month and you are rated 200 percent, your premium is $200 per month. The opposite is also true. If it is determined (via health history declaration and blood and urine tests) that you are healthier than average, some insurance companies offer discounts to the standard price.

5. The insurance company will also ask you about your habits. Habits such as smoking, drinking, and drug use can prevent you from obtaining life insurance or make the price exponentially higher (rating). This is because poor habits usually lead to poor health and a decrease in life expectancy. Your habits also may include your activities. Activities like scuba diving, backcountry skiing, or professional racing of motorized vehicles can also make obtaining life insurance difficult or costly. Activities can sometimes be "excluded" or rated (making the price higher) in the policy. Exclusions and ratings are important

as they allow the insurance company to insure you but with conditions. For example, if you skydive, your policy may be issued with the condition that if you die while skydiving your policy will not pay out. A rating would mean that the policy is issued with a higher price because the insurance company is willing to accept the risk of your activity and you are willing to pay more for the policy as long as it covers your death from that activity.

6. Buy life insurance (or any kind of insurance!) while you're healthy and do not have bad habits. Once a policy is issued, the insurance company can not change the terms of the policy regardless of changes to your health or habits.

There are many different forms of life insurance, but for simplification, they can be classified under two different types.

TEMPORARY OR TERM INSURANCE

Term insurance is issued with a fixed price for a fixed term. For example, you can buy policies that have a price that is level (does not change) for periods of five to thirty years, or even to your age of one hundred. The shorter the period chosen, the lower the initial price of the policy. Choosing a longer-term policy guarantees a longer period without price increases. After the initial term is completed, the policy will automatically renew at a new price (this price is determined when the policy is issued and cannot be changed by the insurance company). The renewal price is normally much higher than the initial price. The renewal price is guaranteed and the option to renew the policy is guaranteed as well. This is important because if your health or habits change and you are no longer able to purchase life insurance, you can still keep your policy if you are willing to pay the higher price. This protects you from losing your insurance due to changes in your health or habits and protects the insurance company from insuring people with poor health or habits at prices that are too low. Term insurance policies are designed to be replaced by new policies at each renewal of the term. Term insurance usually becomes unavailable at age eighty.

Term insurance is for insurance needs that will eventually no longer be needed such as paying off debt or replacing the breadwinner's income. Eventually debts are paid and income needs end (like at retirement).

If others will suffer financially from your early or untimely death (your dependent family members or a business that depends on your skills), term life insurance may be a good option for you. Term life insurance can help your survivors cover any debts you have (mortgage, business loans, car loans) or replace your lost income.

PERMANENT LIFE INSURANCE

A timely death means you died at or after your life expectancy as a male or female. Everyone dies eventually, some before (untimely) and some after (timely) life expectancy. When you purchase permanent life insurance, it is meant to be kept until your demise, regardless of whether your death is timely or untimely. Permanent insurance differs from temporary insurance in that there is no fixed term. The term of the permanent policy is the eventual day of death of the insured. For simplicity, term insurance is like renting the insurance (you have to give it back if you do not die before the term expires) and permanent insurance is like buying the insurance (you own it and it becomes more valuable over time as you age). Term insurance is inexpensive when you're young and gradually becomes more expensive as you age, while permanent insurance is more expensive to buy (relative to term insurance) in the early years but does not increase in price as you age; the premiums may not even be required at some point in time as the policy will be "paid up."

Purchase permanent insurance for certain eventualities like funeral and final expenses, charitable giving, estate planning, and estate taxes. When appropriately structured, permanent life insurance is one of the best strategies to efficiently transfer wealth from one generation to the next. It is one of the only ways to reduce the amount of taxation paid when a person dies. This leaves more money for those left behind.

When used properly, permanent life insurance can also be a powerful wealth creation tool, both for the insured and for the beneficiary. The tax treatment of deposits inside a permanent insurance policy are quite attractive. Policy owners are allowed to deposit extra funds into the policy that may be exposed to a variety of investment choices. The amount that you can use for extra deposits is limited by government regulations once the money is inside the policy. The investment portion of the policy is no longer subject to taxation. The owner of the policy can also access the funds inside the policy tax-free by using the value of the policy as collateral for a loan.

Proceeds from insurance policies pay a tax-free benefit upon the insured's death. Creating wealth inside a permanent life insurance policy is for people with no short-term debt and who have retirement savings plans and tax-free savings accounts maximized where appropriate. When you have exhausted all other forms of savings, complex insurance strategies can be explored with the help of an experienced trusted financial advisor.

ADVISOR WATCH

Unfortunately for the insurance industry, professional advisors, and the average consumer, complex insurance strategies are marketed primarily to financially uneducated people by financially ignorant salespeople masquerading as financial advisors, creating terrible outcomes. These schemes are promoted because they generate big commissions off the backs of ordinary people with little or no consequences to the promoters. Commissions are much larger on permanent insurance sales than on term insurance sales. Multilevel marketing companies offering "financial planning" are the biggest offenders of this problem. These salespeople rarely have any industry education other than passing the life insurance licensing tests, and they rarely have any financial planning designations like the CFP™ designation or the CLU® (Chartered Life Underwriter) designation. There is nothing wrong with supporting new insurance agents with your business, but avoid agents associated with national multilevel marketing companies and quickly walk away if the agent is recommending complex products.

Investing money inside an insurance policy is an excellent option for wealthy families who have no debt and have their retirement savings plan savings and their tax-free savings accounts maximized. Investments inside insurance contracts are not able to be withdrawn without significant tax issues.

Between 80 and 85 percent of people who start a career selling life insurance will quit in the first three years.

CHAPTER 19

CRITICAL ILLNESS INSURANCE MADE EASY!

LOUSY OUTCOME

Suzie and Amit were married, were in their late thirties, and had two children. Suzie made very good money as a public speaker. She would typically speak fifty times a year at $5,000 a pop. Amit stayed home with the kids and took care of Suzie's company bookkeeping. They met with an insurance agent to purchase life insurance to pay off their mortgage if either of them died prematurely. The agent completed an insurance needs analysis on the family. The agent recommended the right amount of life insurance for each of them and recommended a long-term disability policy on Suzie, as she was the primary breadwinner. The agent also recommended a critical illness policy on Amit because he had no other safety net and would not qualify for a long-term disability policy, as he had no income. Amit and Suzie declined the critical illness policy on Amit; they decided the premiums for all this new insurance were just too high (even though they could have easily afforded them). A few years later, Amit survived a stroke but needed to be cared for twenty-four hours a day, seven days a week. Suzie wanted to make sure she was taking care of Amit and her children, so her ability to do her speaking engagements was limited, and her income was cut in half. Suzie also hired a caregiver for her family when she was away, so their expenses were much higher. Suzie was unsure how long they could manage this and worried about their future.

GREAT OUTCOME

Suzie and Amit agreed with the agent's assessment that Suzie's income might be at risk if Amit could not care for himself or their children. Suzie and Amit also purchased a $250,000 critical illness policy on Amit as the agent recommended. When Amit had his stroke a few years later, he received a check for $250,000 tax-free. Suzie used the money for things like additional home care and renovations to allow for wheelchair access. The money enabled Suzie to adapt to her new reality and change the way she earned her money. There was significantly less stress in the household knowing they had the funds required to take care of Amit and the rest of the family.

THE FACTS

Critical illness insurance is a contract between the policy owner (you) and the insurance company. The policy states that for a specified premium (the cost), upon the thirty-day survival of the insured, the insurance company will pay out a specified amount (face amount) of money to the insured or other beneficiary.

The premium or cost of the insurance policy is determined when the contract is issued and cannot be changed or altered by the insurance company.

Not everyone will get sick during their lifetime. Policies can be purchased to be in force for a specific amount of time (term insurance), such as ten or twenty years, or until certain ages, such as age sixty-five or age seventy-five, while other policies are meant to be in force for the entire life of the insured (permanent insurance). The proper type of insurance must be purchased for the proper purposes!

You must be relatively healthy to buy critical illness insurance. When you apply for critical illness insurance, you will be asked to provide a history of your health and your immediate family's health (mother, father, sisters, brothers). The insurance company will determine if your health as it stands right now, and the history of your family's health, will lead you to be more of a risk for a covered critical illness. If you or your family have a history of poor health, such as high blood pressure, diabetes, cancer, or heart attack, you may not be able to obtain critical illness insurance at all. The worse you and your family's health history is, the higher the price; this is called a "rating." When you apply for insurance, you are normally advised of the standard (normal) price. Standard price is the price most people will pay who have normal or near normal health history. If your health is abnormally poor, or your family history shows a high incidence of critical illness, the insurance company may still offer to insure you, but it will offer the insurance to you at a higher price. Ratings can be as low as an additional 25 percent of the premium to up to 400 percent of the premium. For example, if the standard premium is $100 per month and you are rated 200 percent, your premium is $200 per month.

The insurance company will also ask you about your habits. As with life insurance, habits such as smoking, drinking, and drug use can prevent you from obtaining critical illness insurance or make the price exponentially higher (rating). This is because poor habits usually lead to poor health and higher incidences of illness.

Buy critical illness insurance (or any kind of insurance!) while you're healthy and do not have bad habits. Once a policy is issued the insurance company cannot change the terms of the policy regardless of changes to your health or habits.

Critical illness insurance has only been around for a few decades, and not everyone has heard of it or understands it. If you have critical illness insurance and are faced with an illness such as cancer, heart attack, stroke, blindness, or deafness, you as the insured are paid the benefit of the policy. For a typical list of covered conditions, go to http://www. moneyadvisor.ca/criticalIllness.

While in the past critical illnesses frequently resulted in death, it is far more likely today that you will survive (at least for quite a few years) an incident of a critical illness. Making sure your finances are not affected if you have a critical illness is the essential purpose of critical illness insurance.

Most insurance contracts require the insured to survive at least thirty days past the initial diagnosis to qualify for the payment. If the insured dies before the thirty-day requirement, no payment is made on the policy. (If the insured also had life insurance in place, the life insurance would pay out instead.) Most critical illness policies have a refund at death option that pays out a refund of all premiums paid if the insured dies (from any disease or injury) without collecting the benefit. Many policies also feature an option for a refund of premiums to the policy owner should there be no claims made; however, this option significantly adds to the premiums up front.

Many advisors recommend a face amount of one to two years of after-tax income, depending on your situation. If you or a combination of you and your non-income-earning spouse earn $100,000 per year after tax, a typical benefit amount would be between $100,000 and $200,000. It is recommended that you have critical illness insurance on both parties.

If you are unfortunate enough to claim on the policy,

the benefit is tax-free and can be used for any purpose. And unlike a long-term disability policy (see Chapter 20), your inability to go to work or show a decrease in income is not a requirement to claim; you simply must be sick enough. Sick enough means that you satisfy the definition of the disease or disorder covered in the policy. If you get cancer, but it is not life-threatening, it may not be covered (you didn't have a bad enough cancer; that's a good thing!). In Canada, most insurance companies have adopted similar definitions of diseases or disorders to help ensure more consistent decisions on claims.

Most employers have added a critical illness benefit or option to their group plans. Most have small payouts as a standard but offer optional additional coverage if the insured can qualify. However, the best critical illness policy is the one you own and control yourself. Creditor (bank loans) or employer critical illness policies may be easier to get and possibly a little bit cheaper; however, you do not own the contract, so the policies can be taken away or the benefits modified at any time.

ADVISOR WATCH

Critical illness insurance is an important part of every family's insurance program. Your advisor should help you understand the effect of a critical illness on your financial plan. If a risk has been identified, the advisor should recommend the appropriate solution for your situation. An advisor who is solely concerned about making commissions will recommend a lower face amount and permanent solutions that significantly increase the price of the policy and the commissions paid rather than the right amount of benefit on a term policy that has lower premiums and lower levels of commission.

CHAPTER 20

LONG-TERM DISABILITY INSURANCE MADE EASY!

LOUSY OUTCOME

John owned a small construction business, was married to Marla, and had two kids. John still did lots of the hands-on labor for the company and only used other tradespeople when necessary. He had no employees. Marla stayed home to take care of the kids, did the bookkeeping for the business, and paid all the bills. John and Marla need about $5,000 per month to keep the household going. They have about $15,000 saved for a rainy day.

When John and Marla went to the bank for a mortgage, the banker explained that John could get disability insurance to cover his mortgage of $1,000 a month for two years. John thought that was a great idea. John also had workers compensation coverage (WCB) as the business owner, mainly because the coverage is required for tradespeople on site at most of his projects.

One day while the family was skiing, John lost control and hit a tree. John broke his back and was unable to work for three years. WCB did not pay him anything, as the accident did not happen while John was at work. His bank happily paid his $1,000 per month mortgage for twenty-four months, then the coverage stopped. Even with the mortgage coverage from his disability insurance, John could not support his family after just three months.

GREAT OUTCOME

After getting his mortgage and hearing about the disability insurance offered by the bank, John decided to consult with a trusted financial advisor to get a second opinion. The TFA met with John and Marla to learn their situation, budget, and goals. The TFA then mapped out a plan to ensure that John had sufficient coverage to take care of the family should he become sick or have an accident that prevented him from working at his regular job. The cost was a little more than the bank product that the teller had suggested but covered the $5,000 per month they needed.

When John broke his back skiing, the insurance that he had purchased began paying him $5,000 per month tax-free after just thirty days of being off work. The insurance paid John until he could return to work and even offered some built-in benefits to help him return to work faster. He took care of his income so his family could take care of him.

THE FACTS

How would you maintain your lifestyle if your ability to earn the income you need were taken away due to injury or illness, on or off the job? You may have savings in place to fund short- or long-term periods of unemployment or loss of income. Everyone should have three months of cash on the sidelines just in case. But what will you do when your savings run out? You may be able to get help from family and friends, but this is not a long-term solution.

Decide if protecting your income is important to you. Is your ability to provide income for yourself and your family worth safeguarding? You insure your car and likely your home if you own it, so why not your ability to earn income? If you answered yes, you should purchase a long-term disability policy; some employers offer long-term disability coverage for their employees as part of an overall benefits package. An employer-sponsored group plan is the least expensive way to ensure your income is protected should you be unable to work due to injury or illness for a prolonged period (usually three or four months). If your employer does not offer this protection, or you are the employer and do not have it, you must purchase it yourself.

When purchasing a policy, you must determine how much money you require monthly to live on and how long you want that income to continue if you cannot work (we recommend to retirement age of sixty-five). You should also determine what features you need. Long-term disability contracts can be customized to the client's specific needs. There are many optional features that can achieve things like the ability to purchase more insurance as your income rises in the future without providing additional health details or the option to receive up to 50 percent of your premiums refunded if you do not make any claims every few years. There are many features that can be added, far too many to discuss in this chapter. The premium for that plan will be determined not only by how much the payout will be but also by factors such as your age, smoking status, and above all, your occupation. The "riskier" your occupation, and the more additional features you choose, the higher the policy's price. The riskier your occupation, the more likely you are to use it. The reverse is true.

One in three people will experience a short- or long-term disability event before age sixty-five. Insuring your income should be thoughtfully considered for anyone who does not have this coverage through their employer.

ADVISOR WATCH

Engaging a qualified insurance advisor is critical when determining the right policy for you. There are many options and details in every product available, and unless you have an expert agent in this area, you may find yourself with either the wrong amount of coverage or no coverage at all when you need it most!

Advisors representing just one company's products tend to fit the client into the product. The product features could be lacking for the individual client's needs. An insurance broker can fit the product to the client by matching the client to the right company's product niche. Avoid a single-product-pushing agent and engage a qualified broker to find the best product for you.

CHAPTER 21

CHILDREN'S INSURANCE MADE EASY!

LOUSY OUTCOME

Jennifer was a teacher, and Cory was a self-employed consultant. Both earned excellent incomes, and both were very frugal. They had two children, Beth and Barry. Cory and Jennifer met with an insurance advisor after Barry was born. The advisor did an excellent job of putting a life insurance policy on both Jennifer and Cory. The advisor assumed that because Jennifer was a teacher and had group benefits, the death benefit for each of their children automatically put in place by the group plan was sufficient, so the advisor did not discuss the children's insurance. Fifteen years later, Barry was diagnosed with a very severe case of type 2 diabetes. When Barry got older and wanted to start his own family, he would have a tough time obtaining any life insurance or critical illness insurance on himself, due to his diabetes.

GREAT OUTCOME

When Cory and Jennifer met with their trusted financial advisor, instead of assuming they did not want to discuss insurance options for their children, the TFA educated Cory and Jennifer about the potential benefits of protection for Beth and Barry. The policy that Cory and Jennifer bought offered a child rider, which provided a small death benefit should the unthinkable happen but also had a built-in clause that allowed Beth and Barry to purchase insurance in the future without providing medical information, which was something that Barry could use given his diagnosis.

The TFA also informed Jennifer and Cory about juvenile critical illness insurance that would pay a benefit on the diagnosis of covered conditions like cancer, diabetes, and brain tumors. One of the options available in the contract was a rider that would also refund all the premiums to Cory and Jennifer when the policy matured if no claims were made once the child reached age eighteen.

Ultimately, Jenn and Cory purchased whole life insurance and critical illness insurance on Beth and Barry. When Barry was diagnosed with type 2 diabetes, his policy paid out the benefit they had purchased. Beth did not claim on her critical illness policy, so the premiums were refunded to Cory and Jennifer. With Barry's whole life policy, he was able to purchase the life insurance he wanted when he got married and started his own family due to the built-in guaranteed insurability provisions on his contract.

THE FACTS

Most people do not insure their children to get rich in the event of their child's death. Although rare, the death or sickness of a child is an extremely difficult event to go through. Unfortunately, most children's hospitals are consistently busy helping children get through health challenges, both minor and major.

The purpose of determining whether to purchase insurance for the life or health of your children is about two things:

1. The financial impact of their untimely death or illness.

2. The built-in options that guarantee the right to purchase insurance on themselves in the future without providing medical evidence.

Thankfully a properly constructed insurance plan can provide both.

It is very common for parents or grandparents who understand the value of insurance to consider purchasing insurance plans when the children are young and healthy.

The most basic way of insuring your child is to have them included as a rider or option on the parents' insurance policy. The option is usually very inexpensive (two to four dollars per month per child) and has built-in guaranteed insurability for the children when they become adults or reach certain ages.

The most popular type of insurance purchased for children is whole life insurance. This type of insurance is meant to be kept for the "whole of life." Whole life insurance policies issue dividends every year; more insurance is purchased with those dividends, increasing the death benefit over time. Since the child is young and healthy, these policies are very affordable. Guaranteed insurability is often offered as an option (rider) on the policy that allows the child to buy insurance when they are an adult (or reach certain ages) without qualifying medically for it. Of course, if the child does pass away prematurely, the death benefit will pay out to the parents (or another named beneficiary). This tax-free money can be beneficial as it will assist in making the grieving process more about grieving and less about the financial impact of the death. Funerals, loss of income if taking time off, or other expenses can put a significant strain on families' finances, which is precisely not what loved ones want to be thinking about at this difficult time.

Many insurance companies also offer juvenile critical illness policies that pay a benefit if the child is diagnosed with conditions such as cancer, multiple sclerosis, diabetes, or brain tumors. You can often add the option of getting your entire premium refunded to you if there is no claim made on the policy by the time the child reaches the age of majority or the policy matures. All insurance companies have different features and details; your trusted financial advisor will help you choose the best contract for you.

The decision to insure your children or grandchildren is a very personal one. Still, if properly structured, the insurance put in place early can become a valuable and sometimes otherwise unobtainable asset for the child's future.

ADVISOR WATCH

Most insurance advisors want to sell you as many policies as possible, so when bringing up insuring children, they can be viewed as "salesy," meaning they are just after the commissions. If you have trusted this advisor to put insurance on you, your advisor is likely doing a great job by bringing this concept to your attention. So the "watch" here is that your advisor does *not* bring this up with you when discussing the family's insurance needs. Most people have no idea about the benefits of this type of planning.

CHAPTER 22

INSURING YOUR BELONGINGS MADE EASY!

LOUSY OUTCOME

Kellie and Mackenzie were good friends in their early twenties and decided it was time to leave home and go out on their own. Neither Kellie nor Mackenzie had much extra money, but they needed and ultimately bought some furniture and electronics for their new home. They moved into an apartment on the main floor of a building in a nice neighborhood. Not long after they moved in, someone broke into their apartment and took all their electronics, jewelry, and the furniture they had just purchased together. Kellie and Mackenzie did not buy any insurance for the contents of their apartment, so they had to replace everything at their own cost.

GREAT OUTCOME

Kellie and Mackenzie contacted a trusted insurance broker before moving into the new apartment. The broker suggested a policy for Kellie and Mackenzie to replace anything in their apartment that might get stolen or damaged by fire or flood. In the event their apartment was burglarized, the insurance company would replace everything with new items or pay the replacement costs in cash to them, minus a small deductible. The policy was very affordable monthly, so they decided to purchase it.

THE FACTS

You will likely accumulate assets such as cars, homes, jewelry, art, and collectibles as you go through life, so protecting those assets will likely become a priority.

If you drive a car, you must have insurance. You do not have a legal choice. You must ensure that if you create property damage or physical harm to others while driving, they are protected and made financially whole by you and your insurance company. When purchasing vehicle insurance, ensure that you understand the circumstances for which you would not be covered. Will your car be fixed if you cause the accident, or will the insurance company pay only for the other party's damage?

When renting a home, purchasing insurance to cover the contents (electronics, furniture, jewelry, etc.) is optional.

Should an event occur, such as a fire or theft, and you do not have coverage, you will not be entitled to any compensation from the landlord's insurance coverage (unless it is specifically written into the rental agreement). If you have better-than-average "stuff," you should document the items, have them appraised, and ensure that your insurance company knows about them so they can add the appropriate amount of coverage to replace your belongings. You do not want a cap on the replacement value that is lower than the actual value of the items.

Purchasing property insurance is optional if you own your home outright; however, if you have a mortgage on your home or property, your lender will require you to insure it against loss. Property can be damaged by events such as a fire, vandalism, or weather. Transferring the risk of the cost of these events to an insurance company for a relatively small premium each year will prevent the homeowner from potentially suffering a catastrophic financial loss in the future.

Your homeowner's policy should also include a general liability clause. This clause protects you from others who may want to bring a claim against you should they suffer a loss while on your property. If someone slips and falls on your sidewalk because you failed to clear the ice and snow and they decide to sue you, you will have coverage built into your policy.

Most policies will have something called a "deductible." This deductible is the amount of the loss that the policyholder will share with the insurance company should a loss be incurred. Some losses do not require you to share any of the expense, while other types of losses require a much larger share from you. You may be able to choose the amount of your deductible when you purchase the coverage. The higher your deductible, the lower the premium will be. Pick a deductible that you can live with if the loss occurs. Having a higher deductible prevents policyholders from making small claims. If the deductible amount is higher or close to the cost of the loss, then it does not make sense to file a claim as insurance companies track the claims policy owners make and may increase your premiums with every claim made.

ADVISOR WATCH

The more stuff you have, the more important it is to have a trusted insurance broker to help you put in place a policy that adequately protects your assets. There are many optional add-on coverages available, and your broker will help you decide which options to choose based on your situation, risk, and budget. Shop around or ensure that your advisor has shopped around for you.

Insurance companies price their policies for the business they want on the books. Suppose, for whatever reason, the insurance company would like to reduce its exposure to a specific loss (i.e., insuring too many homes in one area prone to forest fires). In that case, it will increase its price to be noncompetitive in that market. Another insurance company may want to be more exposed to that same market and will price its products competitively. These differences in price mean that shopping around for property insurance is especially important!

CHAPTER 23

WILLS MADE EASY!

LOUSY OUTCOME

Shane and Kristen were married and had two children under eighteen. One of the children was from Kristen's previous marriage. Shane had had the same employer-sponsored savings plan since he was twenty. He married Kristen when he was twenty-five. Shane also had life insurance through his employer. Kristen and Shane did not associate with his parents, as they had had a conflict a few years earlier and did not see eye to eye. Shane's mother did not like Kristen. Shane and Kristen did not have a will or an advisor. One day Shane was driving to work and was killed in a car accident that was his fault. After the funeral, Kristen made claims on Shane's retirement savings plan and life insurance with his employer. The company informed Kristen that Shane had never changed his beneficiary designations on either the retirement plan or the life insurance, and his mother was still the named beneficiary. Kristen planned to take Shane's mother to court to fight for some of the money that she felt she deserved. Shane died "intestate," and now the courts would have to decide who got whatever was left of the money once the lawyers for each side had been paid.

GREAT OUTCOME

A few years ago, Shane and Kristen invited their trusted financial advisor to help them with their financial planning. One of the first things their TFA noticed was the beneficiary designations on Shane's employer plans and suggested they change them immediately. Among other topics, the TFA encouraged Shane and Kristen to get a proper will, especially since there was an extended family. Shane and Kristen took care of getting wills, powers of attorney, and personal directives completed at the same time. When Shane passed away suddenly, Kristen received all the insurance proceeds almost immediately, and the retirement savings plan passed to her via a spousal rollover. Although life without Shane was different, the family moved on. Because Shane and Kristen planned for the unexpected, Kristen could focus on the future and avoid a costly and emotional legal process.

THE FACTS

A will or testament is a legal document that expresses a person's wishes as to how their property is to be distributed after their death and which person is to manage the property until its final distribution. By completing a will, you have ensured that your wishes for distributing your assets are clear and your loved ones do not have to guess or be guided by law to deal with your stuff. The will also provides instructions for the placement or disposal of your remains to those left behind. It's a nice thing to do.

"Power of attorney" (POA) is legal authorization for a designated person to make decisions about another person's property, finances, or medical care. If you become unable to make your own decisions due to injury or illness, having someone to act on your behalf will make taking care of your affairs much easier.

A "personal directive" lets you decide who will make decisions regarding your healthcare and treatment in the event that you become unable to do so. It permits your doctor to act immediately on the instructions of the person you appoint. It also ensures that any special requests you have regarding life support or organ donation will be made known and can be acted upon.

A will is part of estate planning, and for many average Canadians, the will is as much estate planning as they need. It is straightforward: everyone should have a proper will in place no matter what. If you die without a will, you will be considered to have died "intestate." Each province in Canada has its own set of intestate rules. Likely the rules do not reflect your wishes. Dying intestate makes wrapping up your affairs a much more complicated, costly, and inefficient process that is avoidable by having a proper will in place.

There are several easy ways to make a will:

1. Purchase a will kit from an office supply store. This is an inexpensive way to get your affairs in order. The biggest challenge for a "do-it-yourself" will kit is that once it is purchased, it sits on the coffee table and never gets completed or does not get completed properly. If you decide to go this route, ensure that you complete the documents and follow the instructions to the letter to ensure that it is a legal and binding document.

2. Hire a lawyer. This is the most popular way to get your affairs in order, but it can also be the costliest. Suppose you have even a hint of complication in your life such as extended family from previous marriages, minor children or children estranged, or charitable endeavors or businesses. In that case, you need to hire a lawyer to draft your will. Your financial advisor can help you understand some things you should consider discussing before going to the lawyer.

3. Online will services. This is just like doing it on your own; however, you are encouraged through the process, and since you must pay, you are more likely to finish the job. This is an excellent way to get your wishes documented and stored electronically without spending a fortune. Simply google "online will service Canada" to see the services available.

According to a 2018 poll by Angus Reid Institute, most people in Canada do not have an up-to-date will. Do not become a statistic!

ADVISOR WATCH

Estate planning is an essential part of financial planning. Your advisor should encourage you to complete your wills, powers of attorney, and personal directives as part of your financial plan. If your advisor only concentrates on the wealth accumulation part of planning, they are not doing their job.

CONCLUSION

Now that you are armed with the knowledge you need about accumulating, spending, and protecting your money, it's time to find a trusted financial advisor to work with you to help you ensure your financial success.

Accumulating, spending, and protecting your money is not a one-day-only event. If you do an excellent job of just these three skills, you will be financially successful for the rest of your life.

Accumulating money takes time, and knowing how to position money to make more money is a powerful skill, and very few people take the time to learn it. Now you have that power.

Spending money is easy; spending money wisely is a skill. You do not have to skimp on your lifestyle; you have to make the most out of every dollar you spend. Now you have some secrets that most people don't know.

Protecting your money from the events that life throws at you every once in a while ensures that all that great work you did to accumulate and properly spend your money is not thrown out the window if something unexpected happens.

Find a trusted financial advisor; there are a lot of them out there. A TFA will simplify your life. A TFA will help you get your plan for the future in place. A TFA will pay for themself time and time again, just making sure that your plan for your future becomes a reality.

I've shared some red flags and things to watch out for, but here are five questions you can ask when you interview a potential advisor to help you find the right one for you:

1. Are you independent, or do you represent just one company's products? (If they only represent one company's products, they can still be a trusted financial advisor; you should just make sure that any products they recommend are best in class and appropriate for you.)

2. Are you a Certified Financial Planner™ or CFP™ student? Do you have any industry designations? (A lack of commitment to industry education is a major red flag. You would not go to a doctor if they didn't have the appropriate training and education, would you?)

3. Have you had any formal complaints launched against you during your career? (If yes, then do a bit more digging to see if the complaint was legitimate and if it was properly resolved. If there has been more than one complaint, move on to the next advisor on your list.)

4. Can you provide a list of clients that we can contact to ask about their experience doing business with you? (Do not be shocked that the only people on the list are happy people, but asking them about your advisor is still important. If

the advisor is unwilling to supply you with any happy clients to talk to, move on to the next advisor on your list.)

5. What is your plan for succession? Who will take care of us if you pass away unexpectedly or decide to quit or retire? (A planner should have a plan for their clients if something prevents them from continuing to service your needs. A lack of any sort of backup plan shows a lack of professionalism.)

To begin your search for a trusted financial advisor, visit https://www.fpcanada.ca/ and click "find a Financial Planner."

Or visit our website at http://www.kevinmacleod.com/ or start a conversation at https://ipclom.com/contact-us.